WWII
PACIFIC WAR EAGLES
China/Pacific Aerial Conflict *in ORIGINAL COLOR*

Jeffrey L. Ethell

Warren M. Bodie

Color Art by
Bob Boyd

DEDICATION

With the greatest personal compassion and respect we dedicate ths book to the memory of the late Colonel Harry L. Crim, Jr. and his lovely wife Joyce. We were honored to call them friends. Harry flew a combat tour in P-38s with the 14th Fighter Group in the MTO, then went to the Pacific in P-51Ds with the 21st Fighter Group. During the predawn darkness of March 26, 1945, he fought in hand-to-hand combat to repulse the last Japanese banzai charge on Iwo Jima, something not normally required of fighter pilots. He was awarded the Silver Star. The authors came to love and respect Harry during the last years of his life as he served the cause of aviation history with as much determination as he fought the enemy on two fronts. Typical of so many belonging to that unique and selfless generation, he didn't ask for reward or recognition for his efforts. He did it because it had to be done. To be a friend of the colonel had to be one of the true benefits of our profession. We miss you, Harry.

Published in the United States of America by:
Widewing Publications
9017 Stonewall Jackson Highway
Front Royal, Virginia 22630

Registered Office:
Rt. 1 Box 255 C
Hayesville, NC 28904

ISBN 0-9629359-3-X

Book design by Julie Ethell Flournoy and Bob Boyd

Printed in Hong Kong by Pettit Network, Inc., Afton, MN, 1997

Widewing Publications holds International distribution rights. Motorbooks International/Zenith Books holds North American distribution rights to the Trade.

Title Page: An echelon of 201 Escuadron, Fuerza Aérea Mexicana (FAM), Republic P-47D-30-RA Thunderbolts cruise over Luzon in the Philippine Islands on a training mission in July 1945. Based at Clark Field, only one of the T-bolts has the petal paint job on the cowling, and the Mexican national insignia has not yet replaced the U.S. star-and-bar. As the Brazilians had deployed to the Mediterranean in P-47s, the Mexicans were assigned to the Far East Air Forces to help get the war over with. The P-47 was an ideal ground attack aircraft for the theater, able to carry enough firepower to please any ground commander. *USAF*

Page 1: The air war against Japan was forever fixed in the minds of the American public by Claire Chennault's American Volunteer Group, better known as the Flying Tigers. Though the AVG's pilots and crews were recruited before the attack on Pearl Harbor, they did not enter combat until late December 1941. Flying Curtiss 81A-2 Tomahawk IIs originally set aside for the Royal Air Force, the AVG was a bright light in a very dark place during that first six months of war in China and the Pacific. These talented U.S. Army and Navy pilots, having resigned their commissions to fly for China, flew combat for only six and a half months but achieved one of the most impressive kill rates of the war. This patrol mission along the China-Burma border on May 28, 1942, is being flown by AVG 3rd Squadron "Hell's Angels" Leader Arvid "Oley" Olson (flying Chuck Older's No.68), Bill Reed, Tom Haywood, Bob Prescott and Ken Jernstedt. The formation, which included R.T. Smith with his camera, was heading northeast toward Pao Shan near the Salween River to intercept a possible Japanese bomber formation. *R.T. Smith*

Page 2: Boeing B-29 Superfortresses became the symbol of America's ability to take the war to the Japanese homeland and bring the bitter conflict to an end. Initially deployed to the China-Burma-India Theater, the Superfort was, from the onset, a great disappointment to Army Air Forces Chief Hap Arnold, who had procured more money – an astonishing $3 billion – for it than any single wartime program regardless of service. He was not about to call it quits so, in his typical fashion, he retained complete operational control of the B-29 and transferred it to the Pacific. Sticking doggedly to AAF high-altitude precision bombing doctrine, Haywood "Possum" Hansell could not get results with his Superforts, yet he dogmatically refused to change tactics. Arnold quickly replaced him with Curtis E. LeMay, a veteran of the bomber war over Germany. LeMay, in a leap of courage, perhaps recognizing the RAF had some good sense, brought the '29s down below 10,000 feet at night to hit their targets. The campaign changed complexion overnight and Japan was reduced to cinders. These 9th Bomb Group B-29s are climbing out from Tinian in the spring of 1945...the lower left aircraft carries yellow/black flight leader bands. *K. Browne via Norm Malayney*

TABLE OF CONTENTS

FOREWORD

Marion E. Carl
Major General, USMC (Ret)

The Pacific air war is a big subject, only partly because it was conducted across the biggest ocean in the world. While I was directly involved on and off for almost three years, there were thousands of other Marine, Navy, and Army pilots and support personnel who have their own stories to tell.

When Pearl Harbor was attacked, I was flying Brewster Buffaloes in VMF-221 at San Diego. We were immediately sent to Midway, where we waited for six months until the Japanese attack. By then my six-plane division had received Grumman F4F-3s, and the Wildcat remained my airplane throughout 1942.

It's true that neither the Buffalo or the Wildcat was technically a match for the main Japanese fighter, the Mitsubishi Zero. I got through my first combat, thanks in part to the F4F's rugged airframe, and managed to shoot down an unwary Zero pilot who probably thought everything was going his way. In large part it was, because VMF-221 lost 14 pilots and 15 planes. Later that morning, Captain Bill Humberd and I were the only ones to respond to the report of another Japanese raid – fortunately a false alarm.

The Brewster gained a terrible reputation based on that one event, but it's probably undeserved. Personally, I liked the F2A because it was lighter and somewhat faster than the F4F.

Its main fault was poor carrier suitability, which was largely irrelevant to Marines.

Less than three months later I was on Guadalcanal flying six-gun F4F-4s in VMF-223. The Wildcats were relatively simple machines which kept us in business, thanks to superior efforts of our maintenance personnel. We also relied on the coast watchers farther up the Solomon Islands, who usually gave us the 45 minutes warning we needed to meet incoming Japanese bombers. Though it was heavier than the F4F-3, the newer Grumman had no more power. So we really needed to be at altitude before engaging enemy aircraft.

When I took the squadron back for a second tour, we were equipped with Vought F4U-1s. As far as I'm concerned, the Corsair was head and shoulders above most other fighters of its day. With the same six .50 calibers, we now had an honest 400 mph airplane with combat performance and the range to take the fight to the enemy. My last two victories were scored in F4Us during strikes against the Japanese base at Rabaul, New Britain, but mainly I remember flying with Charles Lindbergh, who visited us as a "tech rep" of United Aircraft. He probably knew as much about the Corsair as anybody, and passed along his knowledge where it was needed most.

I'm reminded of other people who fought

the air war. I'd say that most of the pilots I knew in my two combat squadrons were reasonably well trained as far as basic aviation skills. But at Midway, relatively few of them really wanted to be in fighters. Unless a pilot likes to put an airplane on its back, he should do something else. I always loved aerobatics, and since I grew up shooting, I guess it was logical that I became a fighter pilot.

What made the difference, of course, was leadership. In San Diego I tangled with 221's flight (operations) officer, then Captain Harold "Joe" Bauer, who was perhaps the finest pilot in the Marine Corps. Later, when he took VMF-212 to the Pacific, he had done such a good job that several of his pilots were loaned to other squadrons at Guadalcanal. I had the pleasure of flying with Joe on one mission when he shot down three airplanes, and I was about as happy over it as he was! It was a major loss to us when he disappeared in "The Slot" that November, despite the best efforts of Joe Foss and Joe Renner to find him.

My CO in 223 was John L. Smith, who we usually called "Smitty." It was his first command, but he did a superb job. He was very much a no-nonsense type of individual, totally dedicated to getting the job done, regardless of what it took. He was also an excellent fighter pilot, and led by example.

That same quality was evident in most other COs at Guadalcanal: Dick Mangrum of VMSB-232, Bob Galer of VMF-224, and Duke Davis of VMF-121, for instance. They proved that we could overcome the enemy's technical and numerical advantages with proper application of tactics.

Attitude had a lot to do with making aces. Some pilots looked at a big formation of Japanese planes and thought, "Oh my gosh, we're outnumbered!" There were others – Joe Foss is a great example – who saw the same thing and licked their chops: "Boy, look at all those targets!"

That was one advantage of fighting on the defensive as we did at Guadalcanal. Frequently there were enemy aircraft overhead, and sometimes we had to shoot them down just so we could land. However, we lacked the range and the numbers to provide escort for the bombers. By the time I got back in 1943, the F4U had changed all that, and it made a difference in the progress of the war.

My subsequent assignment was the Naval Air Test Center at NAS Patuxent River, Maryland. I felt that flight test was the next best job to combat, and I was fortunate enough to have two

ABOVE: A flight of VF-11 Grumman F4F Wildcats climbs out over the Solomons on a combat air patrol, spring 1943. The nearest aircraft, No.14, carries the squadron's new dark blue cowling, an early attempt at restoring some unit color to U.S. Navy aircraft. As Fighting Eleven pilot Charlie Wesley recalls, "While our Air Group was enroute from the West Coast to Pearl Harbor in 1942, the aircraft carrier to which we were assigned was sunk, so we were on the island of Maui from November 1942 to March 1943. The carrier *Long Island* took us to the Fiji Islands where we stayed at Nandi for about a month. On 25 April 1943 we flew from Nandi to Espiritu Santo, about a five-hour flight. The next day we flew to Guadalcanal, about another five-hour flight. We were on a strip located east of Henderson Field, the Marines on one end and the Navy on the other end. Any time there was a scramble, it was a mad rush to see who would get a fighter on the end of the strip first. If the Marines did, we had to wait until they all took off. Same for the Marines if we got to the end of the strip first. When the Marine F4Fs were replaced by F4Us, we always waited until they all had taken off. In the middle of July we were relieved and sent back to the States." *Charles V. Wesley*

tours there. Flying new production and experimental aircraft kept me up to date with aeronautical progress, and even as a general officer in Vietnam I was able to log missions in A-4s, F-4s, and F-8s, as well as helicopter gunships.

While I thoroughly enjoyed nearly 14,000 hours of military flight time, there's no doubt that World War II was the most memorable period. That's why I'm pleased to endorse Jeff Ethell's new Widewing Publications book, which is a remarkable collection. He has become the acknowledged expert on 1940s color photographs of military aviation, and I think this volume will remain a collector's item in years to come.

RIGHT: Maj. Marion E. Carl, USMC, posed for the camera when he had a total of 17 victories (he would finish the war with 18.5). As a captain, he made the first kill of the Battle of Midway and became the first Marine Corps ace during the bitter fighting over Guadalcanal. Carl was dubbed "the ultimate fighter pilot" by his contemporaries due to his keen sense of what today would be called situational awareness. Regardless of the pandemonium around him, he seemed to have a basic instinct for prevailing in aerial combat. This ability stayed with him through a remarkable career as the first Marine to be designated a helicopter pilot, the first Marine to land a jet on an aircraft carrier and commander of the first Marine jet squadron. In August 1947 he set a world speed record, 650.6 mph, in the Douglas D-558-I Skystreak and a world altitude record, 83,235 feet, in August 1953 flying the Douglas D-558-II Skyrocket. He retired from the Marines in June 1973 after flying over 250 different types of aircraft, defining the term "Hero." *National Archives*

ACKNOWLEDGEMENTS

Without the many generous contributions from veterans and fellow historians, none of my World War II color books would be possible. Certainly *WWII Pacific War Eagles* is no exception. This book is particularly exciting for me since, initially, I wondered how much color of the war in China and the Pacific I could find. As I have discovered so many times before, I shouldn't have worried since there's plenty for more volumes.

May this effort stand in tribute for the generousity of Alexander M. Adair, John W. Althouse III, George Armstrong, Harley E. Barnhart, Carroll S. Barnwell, William H. Bartsch, Henry C. Beck, Bill Bielauskas, Peter M. Bowers, Edward Branning, John Campbell, Marion Carl, Jack Cook, Dennis Glen Cooper, Larry Davis, William M. Derby, Betty Edsall, Glen R. Ellis, Maurice J. Eppstein, George J. Fleury, Joseph M. Forster, Thomas J. Fritz, Jim Gorman, Ted Griber, Lon Hardy, Frederick H. Hill, Glenn R. Horton, Jr., Frederick A. Johnsen, Bob and Leona Kastner, Inez Kuhn, Library of Congress Research Staff, Lockheed Martin Photo Archives, David Lucabaugh, R. Mann, George E. Militz, Jr., Frederick Mollwitz, National Archives Still Photo Research Staff, Norm Malayney, Robert Maxwell, Sen. John McCain, John E. McLennan, David W. Menard, National Air and Space Museum Library Research Staff, Merle C. Olmsted, John W. Phegley, Stan Piet, Frederick J. Poats, Hank Redmond, Duane J. Reed/U.S. Air Force Academy Library, William A. Rooney, Fred Roos, George Saylor, Edward H. Simpson, Jr., Brad and Dianne Smith, Donald A. Soderlund, Jr., Jim Sullivan, Barrett Tillman, U.S. Air Force Photo Archivists, Paul Vercammen, James G. Weir, Charles V. Wesley, Scott A. Willey, Robert E. Wilson, John Worth and Viola F. Wright.

LEFT: Mission, Texas in May 1943 was a vision of Downtown USA during World War II. Most Americans lived in small communities under the shadow of a war that took their brightest and best young men ...and women. Cars were, on the whole, older models often driven to their last mile on regrooved bald tires. The kids riding on the running boards of the jalopy in the middle of the street were happy to get a ride at all. The Humble service station on the left was greatly limited in the fuel it could sell and many cars simply sat in the front yard waiting for better times. With a fierce determination, Americans almost universally pulled together to win a war they didn't start. *John W. Phegley*

INTRODUCTION

Warren M. Bodie

Flying Aces! For massive numbers of boys – and a microscopic cadre of girls – that 1930s magazine title and catch phrase provided a small window of encouragement through which to view the world during a long period of financial deprivation. The Great Depression years of the decade loomed large, sparing few and heaping rewards on even fewer. Aviation had provided optimism and inspiration during the so-called *"Roaring Twenties of Aviation"* through the exploits of some World War I ace pilots and a handful of civilian daredevil "aces" who seemingly cherished fame and fortune more than their own lives. A few daring aviators like Charles Lindbergh had generated great interest in the career possibilities of aeronautics. The motion picture industry, hardly out of infancy, was quick to exploit the thrills and chills associated with flying, and aeronautical subject magazines were quick to proliferate.

Although *Flying Aces* magazine was hardly a step above the normal pulp magazines in quality, it provided a nice balance of factual…well, to some extent…articles, modeling features, fiction and a reasonable number of photographs and line drawings. A series of fiction stories, for example, related the exploits and harrowing experiences of a heroic flyer of exceptional ace caliber – a man dedicated to the single-minded defense of America at all costs. That character was given the name "Buzz" Benson, as I recall, and was a probable relative of "Batman" or yet another fictional aviator who was, I believe, named Kerry Keen. No peril was too great for them to face. As the activities of a WWI aviator known as G-8 became more outlandish and improbable during the 1930s, the interest in "Buzz" and the Bill Barnes Air Adventurers grew. There was no longer a fundamental constraint of WWI period aircraft. Benson was a favorite of mine for one specific reason: his battles were with a specific class of enemy. The simple fact I believed implicitly that such battles were inevitable merely multiplied my interest.

Since my father and all my uncles had been heavily involved in the military activities of WWI, it was only natural I was a sincere student of military history. The Nostradamus type prognostications of the author who created the indomitable "Buzz" Benson centered on Japanese expansionism in Asia and the Western Pacific Ocean areas. Oh, it was most certainly fiction. What did Americans have to fear from those blatant copycats who were over the horizon, at least 10,000 miles away? That was the same mentality so pervasive in British and American intelligence organizations and in Congressional and State Department circles…just to name a few who saw no potential threat in far away Japanese transgressions. In all those years between 1933, when Germany and Adolf Hitler began to rattle sabers, and the spring of 1940 as we were blasted day after day by radio and newspaper reports of Allied defeats on every front, probably less than ten percent of Americans believed war with Japan was inevitable. Far fewer could conceive of the Japanese being capable of attacking any part of the United States, let alone defeating this nation.

But in the fiction story pages of *Flying Aces* magazine, combat of sorts was already occurring in the far reaches of the Pacific Ocean between a handful of Americans and the might of Japan's air arms. While William R. Hearst's popular Junior Birdmen of America had long since begun to fade slowly away, many of the contemporary teenage members were acutely aware that air war in the Far East was no longer mythical or impossible. To them, there were too many real signs to ignore. This was in an era when military personnel, even pilots with their enviable silver wings gleaming, were loathe to be seen in town in uniform. Warm receptions from civilians were something yearned for, rarely encountered. That feeling was soon to be reversed at flank speed.

One outspoken aviation writer in the '30s - and a fine one he was - wrote a most impressive column and editorials for *Aero Digest*. His by-line was Cy Caldwell. The famed Al Williams, another flier/writer like our own Jeffrey Ethell, was rarely observed retreating from an established position. As it was with the stories in *Flying Aces*, numerous magazine paragraphs flew the earliest storm warnings of what was to come. How could these men have known what was likely to happen? They observed, and they paid attention to the clear signs. They may well have been America's real intelligence agency – like Charles Lindbergh could have been, had he not been obsessed with avoiding "foreign entanglements" at all costs. A zealot – and, as Anne Lindbergh once said, "Too stubborn to listen," – he did not use his God-given charm to make his point. The Nazis and the Japanese soon made it for him. Hearst handled it better; he lured thousands, many thousands, of us into a realistic fold as Junior Birdmen of America, so we were – for the most part – prepared for what was essentially unavoidable, and it came to pass.

Another factor had little impact on the world between the beginning of hostilities in 1939 and V-J Day. But the significance of that factor is fully evident in the pages of this book and, for that matter, in all Widewing Publications books. It was the opportune development of fantastic color film for general use in cut film and rollfilm cameras. A very impressive collector's edition of the French magazine *L'Aeronautique*, issue No. 235 for December 1938, provides a clue about the state-of-the-art in periodical publication at that time. Spectacularly illustrated and printed on slick art paper, it did not feature even one color photograph. Not one! Published in August 1939, immediately before Germany's *Wehrmacht* fired the first shot in World War II, *Aero Digest* issued a special edition commemorating the thirtieth anniversary of U.S. Army aviation, but again there was not a single color photograph anywhere, not even in the most expensive ad.

Inasmuch as Eastman Kodak had launched Kodachrome I in 1938, we might well have expected to see a great deal of such color in another special edition of *Aero Digest* in February 1940 – this one devoted to naval aviation – but such was not the case. Not even on the cover. However, United Aircraft Corp. gave us a very early insight about the future with a Hamilton Standard propeller ad in full color, a photograph most likely taken by Rudy Arnold or Hans Groenhoff, two New Yorkers who were pioneers in using color in their work. But magazine publishers were not quite ready to spend the money required to purchase the photographs and print them in color. (Just to bring tears to your eyes, that magazine with its good paper, many illustrations and top-level writing had no fewer than 172 pages and was priced at 35 cents. But, then again, a new 1940 Ford five-passenger V-8 convertible delivered in Detroit cost less than $1000, tax and license included.)

As war raged in Europe and the Atlantic Ocean and isolationists of every cloth fought to prevail in the United States, *Fortune* magazine – much deserving of that bold emphasis – produced (not just published) an incredible issue devoted to Air Power in March 1941. Although Oldsmobile, Packard, Pittsburgh Industrial Finishes (paint) and other major firms still were saddled with black & white or *tinted* ads, Monsanto Chemicals, Chevrolet and some others led the way with color photographic ads.

The one I like best is a color photograph of one of us "ancient pelican types" in an American Cyanamid ad bearing this prophetic caption header: "Color makes a difference, doesn't it!" And that marvelous issue of *Fortune*, priced at a staggering $2.00, featured dozens of color photographs of airplanes and allied subjects. Even a wonderfully tasteful front cover worthy of kings and presidents was based on a color photo by Robert Yarnall Richie. Well, certainly such things were expected from the old Time, Inc., and Henry R. Luce.

My copy of that pace-setting issue is, like this writer, rather dog-eared now, and in retrospect I wish I had encased it in hard covers. But, it is still probably priceless.

By now I trust you have seen the point of this retrospection, namely the part magazines (and certainly, books) played in preparing many of us for the war that did come, even as the isolationists steadfastly maintained the stance about the war, "Ignore it, and it will not touch us." The publications also thrust us forward into a new world of gorgeous color – albeit one that was subject to some powerful delays. Probably as a result of a sort of war fatigue, aviation photographs (especially color) slid nearly into oblivion for more than a decade. But a handful of us were just catnapping or, perhaps, playing possum. Widewing Publications came alive in this last decade of an astonishing century, dedicated to bringing to life all the superlative color so rarely seen during WWII and in subsequent decades. From first-hand experience, I can assure you that the global war was not occurring in black and white. Relish these *original-color* illustrations now, and stand by for yet more to come.

ABOVE: While the Battle of Britain was being fought on the other side of the Atlantic Ocean in July 1940, U.S. Naval Reserve pilots were flying these antiques – Curtiss SBC Helldivers and a Berliner-Joyce OJ-2 (right) – at USNR Aviation Base St. Louis. Although the sleek monoplane was the standard for modern air war, American pilots were still flying biplane first-line combat aircraft, assured they could meet the enemy on even terms – particularly the Japanese. Intelligence sources reported the Japanese were known to be nearsighted and ill trained. Universal "knowledge" was they were flying inferior copycat designs. The United States was hopelessly naive as a nation, ill prepared for war, with visions of the "Yellow Peril" from the Far East distorted by the popular pulp magazines of the day. In just over a year and a half, the men flying out of St. Louis would be commanding squadrons a half a world away, fighting for their lives. *via Fred Roos*

OPPOSITE: Waikiki Beach was a distant paradise to most Americans in 1941, remote and protected in the vast expanse of the Pacific Ocean. Few civilians in the continental U.S. had ever heard of Pearl Harbor, much less knew it was home port for the U.S. Navy's largest battleships and four of the best aircraft carriers. Even the soldiers, sailors and airmen serving there thought they were well protected from possible attack. The main threat was perceived as sabotage from the indigenous Japanese population. *James Weir*

PREFACE

When Japan invaded China in July 1937, the American view of Asian technology was hopelessly jaundiced. The prevailing wisdom held that Japanese aircraft and engines were merely poor copies of U.S. designs, therefore not worth considering as contemporary first-line weapons. In spite of the warnings sent back to the U.S. from men like American Volunteer Group leader Claire Chennault and Tokyo assistant naval attaché Stephen Jurika, American and British planners – virtually without exception – refused to believe reports of superior aircraft being available to this potential enemy.

The opening month of the war was a terrible shock to American aircrews and commanders. The majority of the Pacific Fleet was sunk by air power on December 7, 1941, and the Mitsubishi A6M Zero fighter and Nakajima B5N torpedo bomber proved to be complete surprises, in spite of the B5N having entered the fleet in early 1938, followed by the Zero's combat debut over China in August 1940. Allied nation intelligence staffs had dismissed the threats as illusory. The British capital ships HMS *Repulse* and HMS *Prince of Wales* were sunk by G4Ms and G3Ms on December 10, 1941, after sailing without air cover. The Allies not only thought the land-based bombers to be carrier launched, but incredulous

Western observers insisted German pilots flew this "special mission" for their less able Axis partners. Catastrophically evident, pomposity and lethargy were more likely of greater importance in the outcome than the performance of Japanese aircraft. All but asleep at the switch on December 7th, America's leaders had learned nothing from the German attack on Poland and France. No American ever anticipated the dedication of the Japanese to their mission.

This attitude was compounded by the racially motivated perception of the Japanese pilot as a buck-toothed idiot with thick glasses, speaking hopelessly broken English. In reality, Japanese naval aviators of 1941 were among the finest pilots in the world. Their training was so rigorous, only a very small percentage of hopefuls graduated from flying school, the

cream going to fighter units. The average pilot in the Japanese Combined Fleet carrier force had over 800 hours flying time compared to 350 hours logged by his U.S. Navy counterpart. The combination of the Zero and its pilot was close to unmatchable for almost a year after Pearl Harbor. U.S. Army and Navy pilots flying P-39, P-40 or F4F "first line" fighters held the fort against desperate odds, finding the Zero's speed and maneuverability stunning. Dishonest intelligence was paid for with the blood of these ill-prepared young men.

Using Chennault's dive-and-slash attack method, and Jimmy Thatch's "weave" escort technique, Americans managed to break even with their adversaries by avoiding the close-in "free-for-all" dogfight. The only Allied fighter capable of meeting the Zero on even terms was the Spitfire, but it was needed in Europe

OPPOSITE: This North American Aviation P-51 Apache (no letter suffix), on a test flight over the mountains north of Los Angeles in the spring of 1942, was one of the production miracles of World War II. When Britain was against the ropes in 1940 she was allowed to contract the small NAA firm for a new fighter. Fortunately the Army Air Corps required that two of the initial run be kept as XP-51s. On July 7, 1941, long before the XP-51s had completed their flight tests at Wright Field, the newly designated Army Air Forces ordered 150 Mustang IAs for the RAF, armed with 20mm cannon in the wings, and kept 55 as P-51s. Only 93, however, went to Britain. Two were held aside for conversion to Packard-built Rolls-Royce Merlin engines as XP-78s, later redesignated XP-51Bs. By July 1942 the name Apache was dropped in favor of Mustang, which the RAF had chosen way back in December 1940. With the P-51A (Mustang II) the cannon were dropped in favor of four .50 caliber machine guns. The Mustang is a near perfect example of how the U.S. managed, with the help of foreign buyers for its aircraft, to get out from under the terrible weight of isolationism and low production rates so fast after Pearl Harbor. *Alfred Palmer via Library of Congress*

and the Mediterranean where Britain was barely holding its own against the Germans. The B-17 was the only genuine war-worthy bomber in the Pacific after the Pearl Harbor attack; tragically most had been lost in the Philippines during those first months of combat. Even so, the remaining B-17D and early E models were range limited, so their utility over the vast expanses of the Western Pacific was minor.

The Japanese also had excellent ordnance...cannons in their fighters and shallow-draft Long Lance torpedoes for their B5N2 carrier bombers, a revolutionary development which made the attack on Pearl Harbor possible. And the Japanese could fly well over 250 miles (often much farther) to hit targets while American carrier air groups were limited to a combat radius of about 150 miles. Isolationism and the Great Depression had done their scurrilous work. After Singapore fell, the British all but wrote off their Asiatic presence. How could it be otherwise with German threats likely to erupt anywhere, anytime? Spitfires were a precious commodity.

Those invigorating first six months of the war convinced the Japanese the quality of both their aircraft and aircrews did not need to be improved to win what was surely going to be a short war. As a result, their small industrial base would not be taxed to increase the quantity of their weapons. During the first year of the Pacific War, Japan was the only nation which did not quickly initiate expansion of pilot training and its attendant infrastructure. The crushing defeats at Midway, Guadalcanal and the Bismarck Sea quickly robbed the Imperial Japanese Navy of the cream of its pilot crop, not to mention carriers and aircraft. Even the surprising IJN victory at Santa Cruz in the Southwest Pacific cost 140 veteran aircrew, many being irreplaceable leaders.

Only with the full impact of how little they had been prepared for a long war did the nation's leaders begin to expand training and production...but it was too late. As military historian Dr. R. J. Overy stated in *The Air War: 1939-1945*, "Having begun the war with some 3,500 army and 2,500 navy pilots, existing facilities provided only 5,000 pilots in 1942 and 5,400 in 1943. With the destruction of their best pilots in the battles from Midway to Rabaul – over 10,000 were killed in 1942 and 1943 – there developed a desperate shortage." America went from training 11,000 pilots in 1941 to 82,700 in 1943, over fifteen times the opponent's output. During the last year of the war the average Japanese pilot had 100 hours of flying time while the American opposing him had up to 600 hours. With no rotation system, Japanese pilots flew until they were killed or maimed. In spite of being pushed up against the wall early in the war, American services rotated their combat experienced pilots back home to impart hard-earned knowledge to pilots getting ready for combat.

With the introduction of the P-38 Lightning in December 1942, the F4U Corsair in February 1943, the P-47 Thunderbolt and the Allison-powered P-51 Mustang in June 1943, followed by the F6F Hellcat in August, the tide of the air war rapidly turned. American technology and training caught up, with a vengeance. Not only were these new fighters faster than the Zero, they retained the virtues of heavy armor protection and withering firepower. Though dogfighting was still not recommended, an experienced American with a degree from the college of hard knocks could twist and turn with a good Zero or Oscar pilot.

While Japanese Army Air Force pilots flying Nakajima Ki-43 Hayabusa (code named Oscar) fighters were not as highly trained as their naval counterparts, they could still give the Allies a rough time. The small "Oscar" was extremely maneuverable and, as with the Zero, had little armor protection or "beefy" structure in order to keep the aircraft light. The Japanese, just as racially blind, expected their moral superiority and disciplined training would never allow the Emperor's pilots to suffer attack from the rear...therefore, no need for protective armor or self-sealing fuel tanks.

Japan's aircraft industry always had a num-

OPPOSITE: The disintegration of Japanese airpower was fixed before the war began due to a number of factors. In the end, nothing could compete with a massive industrial nation which harnessed not only its work force but created the largest training and logistics organizations history will ever record. These 475th Fighter Group P-38 pilots at Hollandia, New Guinea, in May 1944 look at some of the ruin they inflicted on this Kawasaki Ki-61 Hien (Swallow), code named Tony. Thomas B. McGuire, Jr. (pointing), on the right, would later become America's second ranking ace with 38 victories only to lose his life on January 7, 1945, during a low-level, low-speed dogfight. Ace Franklin A. Nichols, the first commander of the Group's 431st Fighter Squadron, is on the left in front of Lt. Calhoun. These men made the P-38 one of the most deadly of all wartime fighters, using its range, speed and firepower to maximum advantage. Japanese industry, geared for a short war, could never hope to catch up with American quality and production. *Dennis Glen Cooper*

ber of excellent fighter designs in testing, but the Zero and Oscar remained the war's mainstays well into 1944, unable to meet increasing Allied superiority on even terms. In 1943 Japan built 16,500 aircraft compared to 86,000 produced in the U.S. In 1944 alone, America produced more aircraft than Japan's 1941-45 total. While Japan was struggling to refine low grade 90 octane aviation fuel, the U.S. had a flood of 120 octane flowing to every theater of operations. Allied fighter pilots roamed China and Pacific skies at will by the end of 1944.

The Allied bomber war took a great leap forward with the A-20 Havoc, B-24 Liberator, North American B-25 Mitchell and carrier-based TBF/TBM Avenger. Through innovation, often well beyond the manufacturer's recommendations, these aircraft turned into formidable commerce destroyers, airfield busters and long-range military wreckers. Bomber crews faced heavy fighter and anti-aircraft opposition, but they got through, often under an umbrella of excellent fighter escort.

In contrast, the Japanese found their bomber force to be relatively ineffective compared to what the Americans were introducing. While the Japanese Aichi D3A (Val) and American Douglas SBD Dauntless carrier dive bombers entered the war basically obsolete, they were quite formidable for the first year. After that, newer types entered combat but nothing changed in Japan as far as vulnerability. The same held true for the newer torpedo bombers. Fighter cover was a necessity, but the downing of Adm. Isoroku Yamamoto's Betty bomber proved such protective cover was not reliable in every instance.

The twin-engined Mitsubishi G4M (Betty) remained the major land-based Japanese bomber of the war, though hopelessly outmoded by 1944. In the end, the ultimate American bomber, the B-29 Superfortress, brought the fury of air power to the Japanese homeland itself. Nothing could be done to stop the Allied onslaught. New Japanese fighters such as the Ki-84 Hayate (Frank), N1K1 Shiden (George), J2M Raiden (Jack), Ki-44 Shoki (Tojo) and Ki-61 Hien (Tony) were excellent counterparts to their American adversaries. Equal in most respects, they had been given too little priority in replacing the Zero and Oscar until it was too late. Realistically, other less interesting factors...hasty engineering, materials delays, engine development and other aspects of a woefully inadequate industrial base...were the major contributors.

Royal Navy fighter pilot Eric Brown measured the opposing carrier forces by the ratio of fighters each had aboard. At the beginning of the war each side carried about 33% of their embarked aircraft as fighters when compared to dive and torpedo bombers. Within a year, American commanders found fighters to be more versatile, able to bomb as well as protect the fleet, and less susceptible to battle damage. During the carrier battles of the eastern Solomons the fighter ratio was increased to 41%, then up to 60% in the Philippines campaign and, finally, in late 1944 to almost 70% as kamikaze defense became paramount. Fighters deployed aboard more than an astounding 100 American carriers had increased by 400% in just three years. On the other side of the globe the same reality drove German fighter vs bomber production as Allied 1,000-plane bomber raids became a part of daily life.

By 1945 Allied pilots could choose combat at will, eagerly looking for prey, confident of victory. While some Japanese pilots could still put on impressive displays of frantic aerobatics, most were only so much cannon fodder in the famous American aces races that, despite the vast distances flown between encounters, took place during the last two years of World War II.

OPPOSITE: This was about as good as maintenance conditions got in the Pacific...Marine Air Group 14 armorers are hard at work reinstalling the six .50 caliber machine guns in a well-worn Vought F4U-1 Corsair at Green Island during May of 1944. The "Duty Thunderstorm" showed up just about every afternoon at the same time, driving everyone inside or under tarps stretched across poles to avoid the torrential downpour. When it left, aircraft skin got so hot in exposed sunlight mechanics and ground crew blistered their hands when thoughtlessly touching it. Such injuries were not simply inconvenient...they were critical to success in combat since they would keep a man off the line for at least a week in a theater constantly short of manpower. The Pacific these men fought in bore no resemblance whatsoever to the prewar cruise brochures and movie theater travelogues which always seemed to imply there were beautiful island girls wearing nothing but grass skirts behind every tree. *National Archives*

1 CALM BEFORE THE STORM

PREWAR DOLDRUMS TO STATESIDE MOBILIZATION

The Pacific War began, at least in the minds of some American planners, in 1897 when the U.S. Naval War College worked up a potential campaign against Japan, already viewed as a credible future enemy in spite of then-current diplomatic breakthroughs between east and west. When the Spanish-American War established the United States in the Philippines as a significant western Pacific power, obviously in direct competition with Japan, both nations considered war more likely than ever. In 1900, American theorists drew up the plans for an invasion of Japan with the U.S. Navy strategy code named War Plan Orange, a campaign carefully and thoughtfully revised over the next 40 years.

Unfortunately, the U.S. military was so crippled by the nation's post World War I swing toward isolationism and the Great Depression that any realistic war making potential in the Pacific was essentially pigeonholed. Within months after the Armistice, an Army of almost 2,500,000 was reduced to a tenth its size while its Air Service section was whittled down from 20,000 officers to 1,300. With wars perceived as a thing of the past and no obvious external security threat, Congress imposed an uneasy and ill-advised harmonization of Army and Navy missions. Political and military complacency, mixed with strong rivalries, was pervasive.

The National Defense Act of 1920 authorized an Air Service strength of 1,500 officers and 16,000 men (out of an Army of 280,000), but these numbers weren't even close to being realized until 1940. The most vocal critic of the process, Brig. Gen. Billy Mitchell, was court-martialed for insubordination. He simply threw fuel on the fire in 1924 by predicting a Japanese attack on Pearl Harbor, which would most likely be executed on a Sunday morning.[1]

Naval aviation suffered terribly as well, yet managed to beg enough money to build and sail six aircraft carriers (in addition to CV-1, USS *Langley*) under the 1922 Washington Conference on the Limitation of Armaments limits of 135,000 tons. Although Japan's limit of 81,000 tons made her six carriers smaller, she kept pace with, and often surpassed, American carrier doctrine. When the militarists gained control of the Japanese government in December 1936, the Washington Treaty was tossed out. By July, 1937, they had invaded China and by May, 1938, two massive 25,675 ton carriers had been laid down. In September 1939 CV-8, USS *Hornet*, was laid down in the U.S., giving both sides the carriers that

OPPOSITE:The racer of Navy patrol bombers, this new Lockheed PV-1 Ventura flies over the southern California coast in 1944. With a top speed in excess of 300 mph, the PV was a favorite with its crews. Pilots found those great Lockheed ailerons (a trait of all the company's aircraft) to be a big help in low-level bomb runs when some maneuvering was required. Configured to carry at least one naval torpedo, the PV was sired from the Hudson bomber and Lodestar transport. With Pratt & Whitney R-2800 engines giving it a significant jump in capability and performance, the Ventura successfully engaged enemy fighters on a few occasions...top speed was very close to the Zero and Oscar. Unfortunately some of the more famous patrol bomber types robbed the Ventura of well-deserved publicity as it harassed the Japanese across the Pacific and as a part of the Empire Express in the Aleutians. Ventura pilots were looked upon as the fighter pilots of the patrol community since the small bomber took some real skill to handle, particularly with one engine out. *Lockheed Aircraft Corp.*

---

[1] *On two occasions, in 1932 and 1938, U.S. Navy maneuvers in the central Pacific region centered on defense of the Hawaiian Islands – without Army participation. Both times "enemy" carrier forces "destroyed" Pearl Harbor. That experience seemed to be ignored at all levels and was obviously forgotten by all but a few.*

would fight the first year of World War II. While American Navy fighter squadrons were still flying F3F biplane fighters in the summer of 1940, the Imperial Japanese Navy (IJN) was introducing the sleek A6M Zero to combat over China.

U.S. Marine Corps aviation, a branch of the Navy, suffered all the way through the interwar period. From a high of 282 aviators in 1918, many manning the first American flying unit ever to go overseas fully trained and equipped, the Corps was reduced to 43 aviators by 1921. By 1929 the ranks passed 100 again and by 1938 they numbered just over 200. The first realistic try at integrating Marine squadrons into the fleet was formation of the Fleet Marine Force in the '30s with an emphasis on tactical support. It was none too soon.

All American aviation units overseas suffered from pitifully inadequate supply and obsolete equipment. In the Philippines, the Army Air Corps' 20th Pursuit Squadron got Republic P-35As in 1940. Unfortunately they had been taken over from a Swedish buy so all the labels were in Swedish and everything was metric, including the guns. Fortunately the P-35As were in excellent shape and stayed in service without much additional effort, once the ground crews became accustomed to them. When they required spares, mostly due to pilot crackups, they became nearly impossible to keep operational.

New Curtiss P-40s arrived in 1941, but the mechanics quickly discovered Prestone coolant had been eliminated from the shipment. Someone had stupidly decided there was no need for glycol antifreeze in the Pacific! Rations began running low, the heat was unbearable and the humidity seemed to promote fungus and mold on everything. There were no hangars at Iba, so all maintenance was done in the open. The only shelter was at the barracks. Accidents continued in the P-40, particularly after a rain when the 1930s-style grass field turned to mush, until over half had been put out of service. Getting new aircraft was almost a pipe dream.

In the face of a head-in-the-sand attitude displayed by most well-meaning Americans, President Franklin D. Roosevelt, his administration and military leaders were preparing for war. In order get around the Neutrality Laws, Congress passed the "cash and carry" amendment which allowed any nation (implying friendly) to buy weapons and equipment from American manufacturers. Not only did this help Britain, France, China and other nations, hard-pressed to fight the Germans and Japanese, buy armaments, it kept U.S. factories open and solvent in a recession economy. The far-ranging result was an almost instantaneous ability to convert to a wartime economy after Pear Harbor. Quite realistically, that would have been impossible otherwise.

In spite of continual warnings and pleadings from the West, Emperor Hirohito's government refused to consider withdrawing from China. As a result, Roosevelt imposed the first U.S. embargo on war trade with Japan on July 26, 1940. From that point on, despite some intervals when negotiations seemed to raise hopes, war was inevitable unless one side gave in. A month later, on August 27th, the U.S. draft law was enacted, on September 16th the National Guard was mobilized and on September 27th Japan became a third party in the Axis with Germany and Italy. By 1941, events were moving so fast few could keep up with them, while many, like Senator Burton K. Wheeler, seemed to believe we could avoid involvement by ignoring facts. On March 11th the Lend-Lease Act was signed and a month later the USSR and Japan signed the Neutrality Pact.

Senior staff officers seemed oblivious to the provocative actions of the Axis, yet almost to a man those serving in the Philippines, Hawaii and the Pacific knew war with Japan was coming. Overworked, underpaid, short of everything at the end of a long pipeline, Americans out there in 1941 felt abandoned and doomed from the start. All the wanted to do was leave. Tragically, most of them never would. The December 7, 1941, attack on Pearl Harbor and the Philippines sealed the fate of so many who would fight with even less than they had imagined during their "pleasant vacation" in the Pacific islands.

With industry and military training establishments well primed for the inevitable, America shook off its stupor. The worst mistake the Japanese made was clubbing America on the head. That Pearl Harbor attack was certainly brilliant but, in retrospect, the disparity of industrial capacity and manpower determined the end result from the first bombs and torpedoes dropped. America mobilized brilliantly while Japan counted on fighting a short war with what its military forces had stockpiled. A Depression work force, starved for jobs, was put on three shifts to work gleefully 24 hours a day, seven days a week for the most part. The resulting deluge from production and training would overwhelm the Axis.

BELOW: Times Square, New York City, was dazzling on this September 1940 night at 9:48 PM, particularly to someone who had never ventured into the Big Apple. Its neon in motion and string of theaters was a wonderland packed into a very small area. The theater on the right is featuring the popular *March of Time* with specials on *FDR vs Willkie* and *Britain's RAF.* The last months of the heated presidential race are reflected by the neon sign above the street in the center and the RAF was certainly newsworthy as the Battle of Britain was still being fought across the ocean. If one wanted lighter fare, the RKO Palace had two features running, *No Time For Comedy* with James Stewart and Rosalind Russell, and Caesar Romero in *The Gay Caballero.* Lowe's Mayfair featured Loretta Young in *He Stayed For Breakfast.* In the bright light of a New York night, going to war just had to be impossible. Who would ever taint the American dream with such an unpleasant thought?
Henry C. Beck

ABOVE*:* In 1939 the World of Tomorrow was a scientific utopia full of hope and freedom from war, at least according to the organizers of the New York World's Fair. Seen here in September 1940, the Fair's symbols, the Trilon and the Perisphere, appeared in just about every magazine, newspaper or newsreel available. Americans wanted to believe the Fair's optimism, particularly with a war raging in Europe and saber rattling in the Pacific. Some of the United States' latest aviation technology was put on display. Sadly, few realized it represented very little of the future and was already obsolete when compared to the Messerschmitts and Spitfires doing battle over England.
Henry C. Beck

RIGHT: The November 1939 "cash and carry" amendment to the Neutrality Laws and the March 1941 Lend-Lease Act not only resulted in a supply line of aircraft and armaments to our future allies, but they kept the American aircraft industry alive. The Depression and isolationism had all but destroyed the United States' ability to do anything more than hang on as other nations forged ahead in military aviation. FDR's attitude invited the aircraft and engine industries to venture forward. This Douglas A-20A Havoc, seen at the new Long Beach plant, was a direct result of the French Purchasing Commission ordering 100 of the company's secret Model 7B in February 1939. At the time, Douglas had no customers for their 300+ mph attack bomber, so the French order for the substantially redesigned DB-7 was a godsend. Although the Armée de l'Air took delivery of more than 100 out of 951 ordered by the end of 1939, the Germans overran France in May 1940. As the official armistice was being planned for June 22nd, the British-French Purchasing Board, a very successful joint venture in Washington, quickly contrived for Britain to take over the remaining order for aircraft (as Bostons and Havocs) a few hours before all French assets in America were frozen. With all the pain of development funding long gone, the Army Air Corps ordered its first A-20s off the British line in 1940, a very rewarding move. The Havoc became one of the most effective low-level attack aircraft of the war. *Alfred Palmer via Library of Congress*

LEFT: As the 1930s closed, the Boeing B-17 Flying Fortess became the symbol of America's attempt to build a strong military in spite of the Depression and isolationism. The heavy bomber was going to be the weapon of the future, at least according to most of the Army Air Corps true believers who managed to scrape up funding. The MD on the tail of this B-17B (with C armament panels and other changes), on a test flight in 1940, stood for the Materiel Division, which undertook all testing out of Wright-Patterson Field for the Army. The "Fort" was also a tremendous recruiting and Congressional funding tool when the AAC made the wise decision to let Hollywood glorify it in movies like *Test Pilot* and *I Wanted Wings*. With "pilots" like Clark Gable, Spencer Tracy, Ray Milland and William Holden, and girl friends like Myrna Loy and Veronica Lake, who could lose? *via Warren Bodie*

ABOVE:The shape of things to come rarely took more striking form in early 1941 than this initial production B-26 Marauder, serial AC40-1361, at the Martin Aircraft plant in Baltimore. The early company name of Martian applied to the aircraft surely seemed to sum up its spaceship-like qualities, but it was changed to the RAF's choice: Marauder. A very sleek machine, basically a flying torpedo with two massive 2,000 hp engines, the Marauder was a drastic departure from previous bombers, very much like the P-38 was to fighters. The B-26's high wing loading of 51 lbs./sq.ft. meant pilots had to fly "by the numbers" and hold exact speeds, particularly on landing with a final approach of 150 mph, extremely high compared to everything else in the inventory. As the first Marauders were delivered to the 22nd Bomb Group at Langley Field, Virginia, in February 1941, problems surfaced immediately. It would take Jimmy Doolittle and Squeek Burnett to demonstrate proper technique and lower the initially high accident rate. *S.I./Arnold Coll.*

25

ABOVE: Another vision of the future, brand new Bell P-39C Airacobras cruise over a cloud deck on a flight from the Buffalo, New York, plant in 1941. Ordered and designed under the same high-altitude specification as the P-38 Lightning, the 'Cobra was one of Wright Field Pursuit Projects Office chief Lt. Ben Kelsey's hopes for matching European fighter technology. When a new project officer followed an NACA suggestion and ordered the turbosupercharger removed from the design, the P-39 was instantly doomed to underpowered, low-altitude mediocrity. The fighter was actually a delight to fly when it was not overweight and its Allison V-1710 was breathing enough air. More weight was soon added with no appreciable increase in power until its only possible role was ground support, something the Russians thought the small Bell did with great success. *Bell Aircraft via David W. Menard*

ABOVE: These 17th Pursuit Squadron Boeing P-26s and Republic P-35As in the salvage yard at Iba Field, Philippines, were a sad look at the new U.S. Army Air Forces in November 1941. In just a few weeks some of these aircraft, along with a handful P-40s – all obsolete – would be trying to defend a pitifully prepared American outpost against the finest aircraft and pilots in the Pacific. The P-35As, seconded to the Army from a Swedish contract, were built to metric standards without a single English language placard or instrument face in sight. Fortunately, being new, they were mechanically reliable, moreso than the liquid-cooled P-40Bs which replaced them. Although the P-26s were hopelessly outclassed in every respect, many Philippine pilots took them into combat during those desperate weeks after Pearl Harbor. *William R. Wright via Viola F. Wright*

27

BELOW: A brand-new 11th Bomb Group B-17D, one of only a handful assigned to Clark Field, sits across the grass runway from a line of P-35As at Iba Field, Philippines, in the spring of 1941. Living in tents was standard with little in the way of permanent facilities...another preview of things to come in the Pacific Theater. The prospect of war with Japan became so real to Army leadership that more than 75% of the B-17Ds built were flown to the Hawaiian Islands and the Philippines to show Japan the U.S. was not going to allow the so-called Greater East Asia Co-Prosperity Sphere to grow in might without opposition. Unfortunately, most of the aircraft in the islands were caught on the ground in the first hours of the Japanese attack, reducing effective resistance to mere pin-pricks. Japanese fighter pilots, finding the early B-17s quite difficult to knock down, quickly exploited their lack of a tail gun. When the tail turreted-B-17E was encountered, the enemy, like the Germans, quickly moved to head-on attacks to kill the pilots. *William R. Wright via William H. Bartsch*

LEFT: With transportation like this Douglas C-39, life in the Philippines in 1941 was close to idyllic...as long as you weren't a mechanic who had to keep the aircraft in shape with few spares and no shelter. The first C-39s, basically DC-2 derivatives with a DC-3 style center section, tail and landing gear, were delivered to Army Air Corps transport units in 1939. This basic Douglas shape would soon become even more famous as C-47 (sired from the DC-3), which followed in 1940. With 16 seats, C-39s were immediately useful in the early days of the war, ferrying supplies as fast as they could be loaded. In the Philippines, as the situation grew more desperate through December 1941, this aircraft and a few others were pressed into flying survivors out to Australia, leaving the "Battling Bastards of Bataan" (no Mama, no Papa, no Uncle Sam) to fend for themselves until death or capture. *William R. Wright via William H. Bartsch*

BELOW LEFT: Several 17th Pursuit Squadron Republic P-35As taxi out at Iba Field, Philippines, during the summer of 1941. By this time, maintenance of the ex-Swedish contract fighters had become a constant nightmare. The pressure of a potential war with Japan, which all in the islands took for granted in spite of what the diplomats in Washington were saying, open air maintenance and the lack of metric spare parts were taking their toll on morale. Pilots, including 17th Squadron commander 1st Lt. Boyd D. "Buzz" Wagner, were ground looping them on a regular basis until more than half were out of commission. Wagner would later become the first Army Air Forces ace of the war. With the arrival of newer P-40Bs, both the 17th and the 20th Pursuit Squadrons were split to form new units, stretching things even thinner. Iba certainly had stunning scenery but with rations running low, constant tropic heat and humidity, mold growing on everything and fungus infected feet, morale got even worse. There was a single wash basin and shower for 120 men. In his letters home, Bill Wright constantly told his wife "Brocky" all he wanted to do was leave and get home. *George Armstrong*

RIGHT: Grumman's line of late 1930s commercial amphibians found a small niche in America's military air arms. With only a few minor changes, more than two dozen G-21s were procured and painted in Army Air Corps blue and yellow for service in 1938 as OA-9s, including this Goose at Iba Field, Philippines, in the summer of 1941. The Navy got a batch as JRFs. The Pacific area was perfect operationally for the Goose, particularly in air-sea rescue of pilots who ditched aircraft within 100 miles of the coastline. Army pilots in the Philippines also operated the Grumman J2F Duck, though the transfer from Navy ownership was certainly unofficial. After the Japanese attack, these hard working amphibians were pressed into constant liaison work, running up and down the Philippine island chain. When Bataan finally fell, the aircraft were overloaded and then bounced off the water into the air to rescue as many as possible from the grim fate that awaited the other Battling Bastards of Bataan. *Fred Roberts via William H. Bartsch*

LEFT: The Philippine Air Force was flying a number of obsolete types, including the Boeing P-26, when Japan attacked, but this sparkling Beech C-45 was not among them. Though small compared to other staff transports, the six-to-eight-seat military version of the Model 18S was among the most effective for a 200-mph aircraft equipped with two 450 hp Pratt & Whitney R-985 engines. Not only was the aircraft comfortable, but it could get in an out of some very small airstrips while still boasting a range of 700 miles, a much-needed capability for the Philippine Islands. Certainly, like all militarized civil aircraft, they were extremely vulnerable to enemy fire with no self-sealing fuel tanks or armor plate. Pilots became fairly adept at extreme low-level flying in the combat zones. Quite often the C-45 was the only available aircraft to shuttle pilots and crews from one beleaguered field to another to fly what first line aircraft were available. *Carleton Edsall via Betty Edsall*

ABOVE: Downtown Manila in November 1941 wasn't all that different from many American hometowns, even down to the donkey-driven cart. Some U.S. towns didn't have as many electrical poles with wire strung across their streets. In spite of the humid, tropical heat that prevailed across the Philippines, Manila was a very cosmopolitan destination for U.S. military men who were stationed in the Pacific...and a major Japanese war plans objective. A bare month after this photo was taken, Gen. Douglas MacArthur declared Manila an open city on December 27th and led his men in retreat to the jungles of the Bataan peninsula. The Japanese ignored the declaration, bombing the city and entered it on January 2, 1942. More than three long years later, American forces retook the city in March 1945 only to find the enemy had tried to destroy everything on the way out (see Chapter 4). *William R. Wright via Viola F. Wright*

ABOVE: As the war heated up in the Pacific, logistical transport to the war zone became one of the most needed capabilities. Civilian airlines and pilots were quickly put under contract by the military services to perform, essentially, their peacetime tasks. Since Pan American Airways (PAA) had pioneered and dominated transpacific flying boat operations, the company was hired by the Naval Air Transport Service (NATS) to fly Consolidated PB2Y-3R Coronados, like this one being loaded in San Diego in January 1943. The Coronado was originally intended to take the place of its PBY predecessor as a long-range patrol bomber but the old Catalina kept doing such a sterling job it wasn't taken off the assembly line until April 1945. As a result, PB2Y production didn't amount to much more than 220 examples. The 31 San Diego-built PB2Y-3R transports, with gun positions fared over and quite a bit of weight removed, served exceptionally well at long-distance ocean supply and were universally loved by crews and planners alike. *National Archives*

ABOVE: One of the 28th Bomb Squadron's Douglas B-18s sits on the line in the Philippines, ready for duty. Unfortunately, none of the B-18s built in the '30s were suited for much more than anti-submarine coastal patrol so they served primarily as targets for eager Japanese fighter pilots. Looking at this machine, relaxed in Pacific peacetime splendor, it's hard to imagine the B-18 was the winner over Boeing's Model 299 (which became the B-17) during the 1935 fly-off to replace the Martin B-10. Pilots found the Douglas bomber exceptionally easy to fly, as were the company's DC transports, but that was no great attribute in the first days of the Pacific War. With no effective defensive armament to speak of, a cruising speed of 165 mph and an operational range of 850 miles, it had no place in any active war zone. *William R. Wright via William H. Bartsch*

RIGHT: These 28th Bomb Squadron Douglas B-18s, cruising off the Philippine coast in the late summer of 1941, were a hopeless deterrent against Japanese intentions in the Pacific. The 28th's twelve aircraft, based at Clark Field, made up one fourth of the American bomber force in the Philippines, while over half of the bombers in Hawaii were B-18s. During the first attacks of the war, most of these Douglas variations on the DC-2/DC-3 were destroyed and those left did not have the range or the performance to do much of anything against the enemy. The bomber's ungainly appearance and lack of performance seemed to fit the name – Digby – given to it by the British and the Canadians. *William R. Wright via William H. Bartsch*

LEFT TOP: According to the bare statistics, training (in all phases) was more dangerous than combat, particularly if it involved learning to bring an airplane aboard a ship. In August 1943, during night carrier landing practice at Holtville, California, Ens. Magnussen forgot to hand-crank his wheels down with this result. Fortunately, his rugged F4F Wildcat, in spite of the engine being torn off, kept him unharmed but the subsequent fire destroyed the small fighter. He would go on to fly with VF-35 off the USS *Chenango* in the Pacific. Grumman earned its reputation as the "Iron Works" with aircraft which seemed to be overbuilt (that's never possible when being shot at). The Wildcat, in spite of being outclassed by its Japanese contemporaries, was simple to operate, had excellent diving speed and adequate armament to meet, and even best, the enemy for the first year and a half of the war. Incredibly, it was still in production and effective as a weapon in the last days of the war as the General Motors-built FM-2. *Edward H. Simpson, Jr.*

LEFT BOTTOM: Like most of the American fighters responsible for eventually overwhelming the Axis, Vought's F4U Corsair had a long development period (almost three years) from first flight in May 1940 before entering combat in February 1943. U.S. manufacturers, desperately trying to shake the Depression's isolationist effects, fought for every procurement dollar. Not only did Rex Beisel and his team design a very distinctive looking aircraft, but when they hung an experimental Pratt & Whitney XR-2800 engine on it they were gambling in more ways than one. Fortunately, the Navy had enough faith in Chance Vought's past performance and Pratt & Whitney's Double Wasp to order what became one of the finest fighter/engine combinations of the war. The F4U-1, like this one near the Stratford, Connecticut, factory in the summer of 1942, would "make" the Corsair's reputation when flown by a small, determined band of Navy and Marine pilots. *S.I./Groenhoff Coll. via Stan Piet*

ABOVE: First flown in February 1939, the Martin PBM Mariner quickly found a home in U.S. Navy patrol squadrons. The Wright R-2600 powered PBM-3, like this one on a stateside training mission in late 1942, came in a number of subtypes with stretched engine nacelles featuring internal bomb bays, an ideal design feature which kept the designers from having to cut bomb doors into the hull. Several PBM-3Cs and Ds were fitted with a large radome above and behind the cockpit, equipment that would later be a hallmark of the R-2800-powered -5s. With a range of over 2,100 miles while carrying a crew of nine and 2,000 pounds of bombs or depth charges, the PBM-3C was an outstanding patrol bomber. Although it didn't get much publicity during the war, the Mariner was a deadly opponent encountered by numerous Japanese ship captains, particularly at night. *National Archives*

ABOVE: The Grumman Iron Works reputation for great airplanes was solidified by the F6F Hellcat. A simple aircraft to build, maintain and fly, the initial production F6F-3, like this one over the San Francisco area in early 1943, remained the pattern for the entire series with only a few minor changes. After entering combat in August 1943, in almost exactly two years Hellcats shot down 5,174 enemy aircraft, almost 75% of all the Navy's air-to-air kills. The Hellcat was safe, rugged, able to take a significant amount of battle damage and still come back to the carrier. Though not as fast, at 380 mph, as other American fighters, it carried excellent firepower and had that legendary rugged-as-a-bridge construction. Grumman F6Fs, along with Vought Corsairs, dominated the Pacific carrier war. Pilots, who loved the Hellcat's handling qualities, had so much confidence in the aircraft and themselves they complained of not having enough enemy aircraft to hunt down. *National Archives*

LEFT: An F6F-3 Hellcat from VF-5 gets a going over on the deck of the USS *Yorktown* (CV-10) during the new carrier's May-June 1943 shakedown cruise near Trinidad. The large Grumman was new to the fleet so there would be "bugs," but not nearly as many as anyone could have expected. From the start the F6F was simple to keep in fighting trim, ending the war with a close to phenomenal 95% serviceability rate. Like the older F4F, the Hellcat's wings were folded manually rather than hydraulically. This was somewhat of a chore on deck when things were busy, but it cut maintenance downtime drastically when compared to the maze of wing fold hydraulic lines in most other Navy carrier aircraft. Mechanics loved working on the Hellcat. *National Archives*

RIGHT: A yellow-jerseyed plane director gives a thumbs up to Fly Control on a training cruise off the U.S. coast. This means the flight deck officer has received a signal from the squadron leading chief who has checked each aircraft at station Fly 3 as ready for flight. American carriers were divided into three sections where men wore different colored jerseys which identified their job. In spite of the chaos which seemed to reign on a carrier deck, everything was a carefully staged and rehearsed ballet. Certainly things often went wrong, but its quite a testimony to Naval Aviation that the same system, basically unchanged, is used on modern aircraft carriers. Pay was often dismal for such hazardous work, but no service could top Navy food and accommodations. No one board ship would have rather been in a fox-hole or dug in under fire on a beach. *National Archives*

BELOW: Major Dick Bong, with 28 victories at the time, cranks up his P-38J-20-LO Lightning at Craig Field, Alabama, in June 1944 during a visit with pilots on their way to the Pacific theater. He was more than happy to pass on what he had learned in fighting the Japanese since he considered himself "the lousiest shot in the Army Air Forces." He had come home on leave, he said, because he wanted to learn the fine art of aerial gunnery. Having enlisted in the Army Air Corps in 1941, Bong's operational training had been rudimentary, ill preparing him to be a fine shot. Fortunately, he could maneuver a Lightning like few others. When he went to Foster Field at Matagorda, Texas, on July 7, 1944, he reported to several instructors, including Capt. Bill Gunter, who was impressed by Bong's serious, quiet determination. There was no hint of a prima donna attitude and he never used his fame to get by anything. He didn't need to. Gunter considered him one of the finest pilots he had ever worked with. By the time Bong graduated on August 6th, he had put in over 50 hours of flying/gunnery time. He returned to the Pacific for his third combat tour and destroyed another 12 Japanese aircraft by December to become America's Ace of Aces with 40 kills. *James G. Weir*

OPPOSITE: Air transportation made major leaps in capability during World War II, from the twin-engine types of the 1930s to four-engine marvels which could cross oceans with a substantial amount of cargo. Typically, the Depression-era Army never wanted a four-engine transport...until the Japanese attacked in the Pacific. Douglas had developed the DC-4A with five airlines, backed primarily by United and American. Nine were in the advanced stages of construction at Clover Field by December 1941. Early in 1942 the AAF, as it did across industry, requisitioned the company's civilian production line and assigned the next Cargo category type number, creating the C-54. Like the C-47, the Skymaster was virtually unchanged from its commercial configuration and the first C-54 was flown at Santa Monica on February 14, 1942. With a useful load of 25,000 pounds and a range of 3,900 miles, the C-54 brought the AAF into the modern transport world. *USAF via Stan Piet*

RIGHT: The Lockheed series of 1930s twin-engine transports were ideal candidates for conversion to bombers. Hang some more powerful engines, deepen the fuselage for a bomb bay, add some defensive armament and the high-speed, fine-handling PV-1 Ventura came into being. Certainly it was more complex than that, but with so little money to work with, U.S. aircraft firms made do with what they had, usually modifying something before creating an entirely new product. Originally built for the British, the Ventura was ordered as the PV-1 by the Navy in July 1942, along with two other types which were already on the line, the North American PBJ (B-25) Mitchell and the Consolidated PB4Y Liberator. A total of 1,600 PV-1s were produced for the Navy, another 388 went to the RAF on lend-lease, 487 were bought by the AAF as the B-34 Lexington (in reality simply a name of convenience that was seldom used) along with another 18 with R-2600 engines as the B-37. Yes, it was complicated enough that few tried to keep track of what went where. *Lockheed Aircraft Corp. via Warren Bodie*

OPPOSITE: A B-24 Liberator taxies out of its revetment at Mokuleia Field, Oahu, for a training sortie before being transferred to the Central Pacific, August-September 1943. Most American planners were convinced the Japanese would return to attack Hawaii, certainly one of the prime targets in the Pacific, so multiple hardened areas were built on fields across the islands. Mokuleia's main runway was 9,000 feet long and 300 feet wide, with a cross runway of 4,500 feet used primarily by fighters. At this point in the war, mobilization was organized with a vengeance the enemy never foresaw, overflowing in every area of civilian and military activity. With the range and load carrying capability to hit distant targets, the Liberator became the primary heavy bomber of the Pacific War until the B-29 arrived. Few really loved the '24 but Fifth Air Force commander George Kenney found it to be the right aircraft for the right time in the right place. *via Jack Cook*

OPPOSITE: With the coming of war, Hawaii was immediately a crucial locale, something the Japanese appreciated but could do little about after their successful attack on Pearl Harbor. These Naval Air Transport Service Douglas R5D Skymasters on the ramp at Hickam Field were part of a vast supply network which used Hawaii as a hub. Able to fly non-stop from the States, then non-stop again to any Pacific destination, R5Ds, along with other American transport aircraft, were able to keep units on the front lines supplied through a round-the-clock effort. The lessons learned were transferred straight into the postwar airline industry with almost no changes. The Skymaster was, without question, the vision of things to come in a four engine future. *National Archives*

ABOVE: On May 9, 1944, leading Pacific ace Dick Bong came home on leave. Though he had to put up with a month's worth of bond speeches and publicity, he had come home to take his first serious gunnery training. Unknown to most of his contemporaries, Bong considered himself a very poor marksman. "I am not a good shot," he said in an interview at the time. "I have to hit them either straight from behind or from straight ahead...or with a deflection of not more than ten degrees.... I consider it a big accident when I hit anything with deflection shooting." When he got back to the combat zone, he found his skill level had indeed gone up, enabling him to down more aircraft for expenditure of less ammunition than before. When Bong had reached number 40 in December 1944, Maj. Gen. George Kenney pulled him out of the fighting for good and sent him home. Tragically, Dick Bong was killed on take-off out of Burbank in a new P-80A Shooting Star on August 6, 1945. A true hero, he would never have considered himself heroic. *USAF via Stan Piet*

ABOVE: *Rapid Robin,* a Pacific-bound B-24, sits under camouflage netting in a revetment at Bellows Field, at the southeast corner of Oahu, in August-September 1943. After being attacked on December 7, 1941, Bellows was rebuilt and expanded to accommodate the increasing flow of aircraft to the combat zones. Rocks and boulders were incorporated into the concrete to blend the revetments into the surrounding area and when combined with the patch garnishing on the netting, the result was quite effective. Fortunately, it never had to be tested. Aircraft plants in California used the same system, adding fake buildings, streets and cars to the tops of their nets. Had anyone really known how hard pressed the Japanese were after the first six months of the war, camouflage would most likely not have been an issue by late 1943. *via Jack Cook*

RIGHT: In spite of the constant threat of another Japanese attack, Hawaii remained an oasis in the midst of war, a wonderful place to relax before or after a combat tour. Downtown Honolulu still had the flavor of a tropic outpost with beautiful buildings and fantastic beaches, yet having the modern trappings of excellent mass transportation and fine hotels. It was hard to believe there was a war on – just the thing for combat fatigue. Most Pacific combat units staged through Oahu and many stayed there for an extended period for operational training before being released for the Central or Southwest Pacific. The most confusing thing to most first-time visitors was the complete integration of the Japanese into the culture. Were these enemies or friends? Almost all the Japanese residents in the islands were Americans at heart, but nationalism and the internment camps at home kept things very confused. *James G. Weir*

RIGHT: A rarity in its day, a color movie, *Home in Indiana* starring Walter Brennan and Lon McAllister, was playing at the Waikiki Theater in Honolulu when 19th Squadron, 318th Fighter Group P-47 pilot Jim Weir was going through on his way to the Central Pacific and combat. Just about every form of entertainment was available on Oahu, from the most innocent to the most perverse, and wartime tended to accelerate the pace of trying to experience everything. The Military Police and the Shore Patrol had their hands full almost every night of the week and the locals seemed to take it all in stride Every serviceman was aware of his or her exposure to potential death on any day. *James G. Weir*

LEFT: This Women Airforce Service Pilot (WASP) is about to climb into her Lockheed P-38G-10-LO Lightning somewhere in the U.S. The WASPs were a unique band of 1,104 women pilots who volunteered to fly Army Air Forces aircraft under civil service contracts which gave them many of the hardships but denied them most of the benefits associated with military life. After graduation, a WASP would be assigned to ferry just about anything built, become an instrument instructor or tow targets for anti-aircraft training units. By the time they were disbanded in December 1944, forty-one had been killed in the line of duty. Political turmoil was always at the center of their existence as a unit, but most of them didn't care as long as they got to fly those great fighters and bombers. *USAF via Stan Piet*

OPPOSITE: With USN cooperation, Pan American Airways asked Lockheed for a large transport aircraft, and the Model 89 soon appeared on the drawing boards. Although war shoved all civil contracts off the table, the Navy ordered two prototypes as the XR6O-1 Constitution. When the double-deck, 168-passenger aircraft emerged from the factory, fitted with four 3,000+ hp R-4360 engines, it looked as if the future had arrived. However, by the time the first flight was made on November 9, 1946, the war was history. Both aircraft, each grossing out at 184,000 pounds, were assigned to VR-44 and served until 1955. On a run down the California coast, the first Constitution, BuNo. 85163, displays the clean lines typical of Lockheed products. As with so many promising late war designs, the XR6O came too late to enter combat support operations. *National Archives via Stan Piet*

ABOVE: Once American production hit its stride, stateside training bases, like this one block-to-block with PBYs, filled up with more aircraft than anyone could have imagined only a few years earlier. Though most operational training airframes tended to be wornout older models, the U.S. was dedicated to making sure aircrews trained long and hard on the real thing. This combination of production and training quickly triumphed over the Axis powers, which moved in exactly the opposite direction. In spite of its 1930s heritage, the PBY remained an active combat aircraft through the end of the war, not only in air-sea rescue but in long range patrol, aerial reconnaissance and night shipping attack. *William M. Derby*

46

OPPOSITE BELOW: When the 315th Bomb Wing was formed in July 1944, its new Bell-built B-29Bs from Marietta, Georgia, were equipped with a new weapon, the AN/APQ-7 Eagle bombing radar housed in an airfoil fairing beneath the fuselage, clearly evident on this one during state-side training. When the Wing was assigned to the Twentieth Air Force for operations out of Guam in March 1945, it was given a specific target, Japanese oil. Wing commander Brig. Gen. Frank A. Armstrong, a legendary Eighth Air Force leader, used the Eagle and his very highly trained crews from June through August to virtually eliminate what was left of Japan's oil production. Properly used by innovative commanders with the courage to depart from orthodox bombing methods, the B-29 was a deadly instrument of war. *John Worth*

BELOW: By 1944, pilot training was roaring along almost unchecked producing a torrent of highly qualified individuals ready for combat. Robert Maxwell stands proudly in front of one of his training P-38Js in 1944 at Van Nuys, California, where the author's father, Capt. E.C. Ethell, served as a gunnery instructor after his combat tour in North Africa. The rotation of combat personnel home for instruction assignments was a stroke of genius, vastly lowering the rate of attrition overseas. Nevertheless, training was still a deadly business. From 1941 to 1945 the AAF recorded 52,651 training accidents in the continental U.S., resulting in 14,903 fatalities and 13,873 aircraft written off. No nation had ever dealt with such massive numbers of people trying to fly such sophisticated aircraft in so short a time. No doubt there was a fair amount of needless attrition, but no one had a corner on fast, correct answers. The job had to be done and the U.S. did it better than the opposition. *Robert Maxwell*

ABOVE: A fine example of the premier AAF fighter of the Pacific, this Lockheed P-38J-15-LO Lightning cruises over Southern California on an acceptance test flight in 1944. The Lightning had just about the perfect blend of characteristics needed for the long duration missions fighter pilots had to fly in the Central and Southwest Pacific. Twin-engine safety, centralized firepower, long range and excellent speed gave fighter pilots what they needed to fight that war. In spite of its size, the '38 could maneuver with the best of them if handled by an experienced pilot, especially when power-boosted ailerons were added in J-25 and subsequent models. One drawback was the length of time it took to become deadly in the aircraft when compared with single-engine fighters. Most considered it a real Cadillac to fly, typical of all Lockheed aircraft. *Lockheed via Warren Bodie*

OPPOSITE: In late 1943, the AAF asked for proposals on a very-long-range escort fighter with the Pacific Theater and the coming B-29 in mind. By early 1944, North American Aviation began work on what would become the XP-82 Twin Mustang just as the first of the lightweight Mustangs, the XP-51F, was ready for flight testing. Using the F as a basis, two fuselages were lengthened and joined by a central airfoil, with the idea that two pilots could spell each other on the long missions envisioned. As the aircraft took shape, P-51H outer wing panels and Packard Merlin engines were fitted. When the XP-82 finally flew on June 16, 1945, it was clear the war had already passed the Twin Mustang by, another example of an idea whose time had not come. Of the 500 NAA P-82Bs ordered, only 20 were built and two of those were converted into prototype night fighters, the P-82C seen here on a test flight, and the XP-82D. The production line was kept open to supply escort fighters for postwar Strategic Air Command and to replace the P-61 night fighter. On June 27, 1950, Allison-powered F-82Gs made the first three kills of the Korean War. *via Peter M. Bowers*

ABOVE: Maintenance in the Aleutians was a nightmare of cold, mud, snow, freezing rain, frostbite and a continual lack of being able to get anything warm, be it human or machine. Two 54th Fighter Squadron Lockheed P-38E-LO Lightnings are getting quite a bit of attention...the two preheaters with their associated hoses and canvas hoods were critical to keeping the complex fighters operational. A third Lightning, upper left of the revetment, is in the process of being reassembled. Four P-40s are in various stages of rebuild or assembly. One on the far left, with its bent prop blades, shows the results of a belly landing, while the next one probably had a prop strike from a nose-over. One Bell P-39 Airacobra is on a flatbed trailer behind the truck at the entrance to the area and another one is on the left. A medevac Stinson O-49A (later redesignated L-1A) Vigilant at the lower left was a critical utility aircraft for the vast stretches on the Aleutian chain. When aircrews went down, they had to be found quickly or face freezing to death. The ubiquitous Cletrac, towing an Allison engine (middle), was one of the most important pieces of equipment in every theater of war since it could move just about anything, particularly when mired in the mud. On the other side of the field are a C-47 and a Lockheed C-60. Clearly the mechanics are having a tough time stopping the mud from flowing over the pierced steel plank (PSP), another theater-wide problem. *National Archives*

2 IN LONELY PLACES

PEARL HARBOR TO NEW GUINEA, THE SOLOMONS & THE ALEUTIANS

In spite of several blatant prewar actions by the Japanese, the attack on Pearl Harbor was a rude shock to both the American people and their military leaders. With a brilliant stroke of tactical genius, Adm. Isoroku Yamamoto, guided by his talented planners Takajiro Onishi and Minoru Genda, had targeted the U.S. Pacific Fleet with a vengeance...but only after the Harvard-educated flag officer begged his superiors to avoid war at all costs.

Yamamoto had been responsible for moving the Imperial Japanese Navy away from battleships to the aircraft carrier. As Navy Vice Minister in the late '30s, he ordered construction of the carriers *Shokaku* and *Zuikaku*, ships the Americans would not improve upon until the *Essex* class. Once resigned to his nation's move toward war with Great Britain and the United States, Yamamoto would only agree, as Commander in Chief of the Combined Fleet, to initiate hostilities with a carrier strike on Pearl Harbor. He had been inspired by the U.S. Navy's own successful mock attacks against the same target in 1932 and 1938, as well as the Royal Navy's sinking of the Italian battleships at Taranto in November 1940 with torpedoes dropped from outmoded Swordfish biplanes.

In spite of Japan's success, in reality the attack, led by Vice Adm. Chuichi Nagumo, bore the seeds of her defeat. Not only did the blow galvanize the U.S., as Yamamoto feared it would, but none of the American carriers were in port and Nagumo refused to authorize a third wave to hit docks, repair facilities, petroleum storage tanks and other important infrastructure. As a result, not only did the U.S. have its carriers available, but most of the sunk and damaged ships were raised, repaired and ultimately modernized.

Yamamoto had wanted to deliver a fatal blow to the Pacific Fleet to keep it from meddling with the Japanese government's Southern Area plans to grab the oil, rubber, tin and other raw materials Japan wanted from the East Indies, the Philippines and Malaya. The war was then supposed to last six months to a year and bring a hopelessly outclassed U.S. to the negotiating table before there was a need for extensive ship, aircraft and pilot replacements.[1]

The Japanese Naval General Staff's plans for success revolved around one decisive battle. When the unarmored American carriers came west as expected, the Japanese carriers would launch their aircraft to put the American flight decks out of commission. Then Japanese cruisers would move in to attack with torpedoes while the battleships, led by the gargantuan *Yamato* and *Musashi*, would move in to finish off what was left. At heart, the naval warriors of Nippon were battleship sailors who failed to appreciate the mobile, fast reacting, pinpoint striking power of the aircraft carrier as the prime naval independent agent. Since all of the Hawaiian-based American battleships had been destroyed or put out of action at Pearl, U.S. Navy admirals had no choice but to leave their battleship mentality behind and rely on the carrier[2].The attack on Pearl was a clear

---

[1] *The author is indebted to Thomas J. Fritz, one of his graduate students at American Military University, for summarizing Yamamoto's attitudes and methods in an exceptionally well thought out 1996 research paper.*

[2] *On December 7, 1941, only the* Lexington *and* Enterprise *were stationed at Pearl while the* Saratoga *was in San Diego. Overall, including U.S. Atlantic Fleet carriers, the ratio was 10 to 7 in favor of the Japanese...among these totals, the Japanese had four light carriers and the Americans had two. Figures courtesy of Scott A. Willey, Col., USAF (Ret).*

demonstration of what carriers could accomplish in one sortie.

With no plans to hunt down the American flattops, in spite of a 10 to 3 advantage in the Pacific when light carriers were included, Yamamoto sent his own carriers off to support the landing of troops as Japan embarked on its occupation of territory. This set the tone for Japanese carrier operations, giving the Americans, and the British, a much needed reprieve, in spite of Japan's fantastic six months of conquest. At the time, none of this was evident to the Allies, who had their hands full just trying to hold their own against a seemingly invincible enemy. To America's good fortune, its new Pacific Fleet commander, Rear Adm. Chester W. Nimitz, was a brilliant, low-key tactician who balanced audacity with realism. He would lead the Pacific Fleet for the rest of the war.

According to War Plan Orange, the U.S. Armed Forces Far East (USAFFE) were supposed to hold the fort against a possible Japanese invasion of the Philippines for four to six months until reinforcements arrived from the U.S. Such an assumption was wildly optimistic, even naive. Washington's directive, that "the first overt act" must be Japan's, created a defensive posture which robbed the Americans of any effective preemptive action. When Gen. Douglas MacArthur, his chief of staff Brig. Gen. Richard K. Sutherland, and Far East Air Force (FEAF) commander Maj. Gen. Lewis Brereton, received a 3:55 AM confirmation of the Pearl Harbor attack, enormous confusion and indecision set in. How should Washington's strictly defensive attitude be interpreted since the Philippines had not been directly attacked? Only after MacArthur had received confirmation of reports of early morning Japanese attacks on Philippine soil, just after 10:00 AM, did he authorize Brereton to bomb Japanese air bases on Formosa. As the B-17s were bombing up at Clark for the attack, the Japanese hit the field, wiping out 12 Forts and the P-40 squadron based there. Much finger pointing resulted but in the end the debacle has to be laid at MacArthur's feet, more likely than not due to Sutherland's advice to "keep out of harm's way" when the situation called for a profound offensive mindset. A strictly defensive posture had cost the USAFFE dearly.

In short order, the Japanese came through the Philippines like a scythe, destroying most of the B-17s and 64 of the 92 P-40s by December 10th. Those fighters left, suffering from jamming guns and other mechanical problems, were flown by pilots with very little realistic tactical training. Even during a decade of Depression, Hawaii was a relative paradise for officers and enlisted men. No threat of hunger or homelessness, pilots flew in well-built airplanes, and the environment was top drawer.

Brereton took what B-17s were left to Australia and new FEAF commander Col. Harold George, as of January 8, 1942, was left with a total of nine P-40s, two P-35As and one A-27 (a combat version of the AT-6). By March 2nd a single P-40 was left with no reinforcements planned or possible for the "Battling Bastards of Bataan." The remaining operational aircraft, called the "Bamboo Fleet," were a motley collection of civil and military second-line aircraft from Grumman Ducks to Beech Staggerwings, but they flew constantly delivering medical supplies, food and whatever else could be stuffed inside. Finally pushed onto Bataan and Corregidor, fighter pilots became infantry soldiers until surrender on May 6th. Half of the 24th Group's 165 fighter pilots were taken prisoner but only 34 were found alive just over three years later.

In February 1942, Vice Adm. William "Bill" Halsey (only journalists knew him as "Bull"), outgunned and outmanned, took American carriers on the offensive, hitting the Marshall and Gilbert islands, then, over the next four months, Rabaul, Wake, New Guinea and Marcus Island. Yamamoto responded by pulling "heavies" *Shokaku* and *Zuikaku* from the Southern Area to the east of Japan in defense of the homeland. In reality, this was the philosophical turning point of the Pacific War, highlighting the drastic differences between the two combatants. America was going to lash out and strike against the odds, while Japan would pull back and defend, with a far better offensive force, to consolidate its gains.

When the Americans did not attack Japan as soon as anticipated, Yamamoto released the two carriers in early April for operations against the British, the lesser enemy, in the Indian Ocean. Then, under Halsey's command, Jimmy Doolittle led his 16 *Hornet*-based B-25s to Japan on April 18th. The raid filled Yamamoto with so much shame he retired to his cabin and refused to come out, leaving Vice Adm. Matome Ugaki to pursue the small strike force. The Naval General Staff, having lost face by failing to defend the Emperor and Nippon, left their Southern Area obsessions and approved Yamamoto's set piece, battleship-style engagement plans for luring the Americans into a trap at Midway, something they had been very reluctant to do. They also moved up plans to attack New Guinea and the Solomon Islands, then ordered an invasion of the Aleutian Islands as a diversion during the Midway operation. From this point on, Japanese carrier forces would be effectively divided, unable to bring their inherent strength of numbers to bear.

Upon moving south to invade Port Moresby, New Guinea, and land troops at Tulagi in the Solomons, the Japanese fell into the trap of having their codes broken, which would do them irreparable damage throughout the war. A small intelligence team kept Nimitz apprised of the enemy's possible intentions, leading him to initiate the Battle of the Coral Sea, May 4-8, 1942. This first carrier vs. carrier confrontation was considered a draw, with each side losing one carrier, but the Japanese recalled their Port Moresby invasion force. Had Yamamoto sent more than two heavy carriers to do battle here, the Moresby invasion would most likely have succeeded and the damage to the limited American fleet been far greater. This would have had far reaching effects one month later during the Battle of Midway. Code breakers once again allowed Nimitz to outmaneuver Yamamoto, who had – a second time – split, and thus weakened his fleet.

The idea was to: 1) occupy the island of Midway and, 2) lure the American fleet into the hoped-for 1905 Tsushima-style single, big set-piece battle. Genda immediately opposed the priorities, asserting the capture of Midway should be secondary to sinking the American carriers, and that the Aleutian force should join Nagumo's Midway force. Code breaking, and the predictability of what was, essentially, a supporting invasion flotilla instead of a free-roaming strike force, sealed the fate of Japan. In reality, the twin objectives of invading Midway and crushing the U.S. Pacific Fleet were, as historian Gordon Prange wrote, "fundamentally incompatible." Yamamoto would split his forces not once, but twice, then send them off on an overly complex pattern of diversion and maneuver. In spite of having more carriers, better quality aircraft and more experienced air crews, Yamamoto lost the Battle of Midway, June 3-6, 1942, and with it the Pacific War. The blame must rest squarely at his feet. Slogging through the Aleutians, a campaign which lasted from June 3, 1942, until August 15, 1943, took a horrendous toll on both sides, more often due to the miserable weather. The Japanese simply withdrew and went home, something they rarely did without an enormous fight.

Two months after the "miracle at Midway," the U.S. invaded Guadalcanal, Solomon Islands, on August 7, 1942, and opened the first American offensive of the war. This small patch of real estate was crucial in consolidating the U.S. attempt to push the enemy back. From the beginning, air power – in particular the small "Cactus Air Force" made up of ill-supplied Marine, Navy and Army fighter pilots – made the difference in holding the island. The third carrier-vs-carrier engagement in history, the August 22-25 Battle of the Eastern Solomons, resulted in the Japanese losing the small carrier *Ryujo* and moderate damage to the *Enterprise*, which had to land her aircraft on Guadalcanal. During the Battle of Santa Cruz 500 miles north on October 25th, four Japanese and two American carriers duked it out, resulting in additional damage to the *Enterprise* and sinking of the *Hornet*. The real loss to the Japanese was the core of their prewar Imperial Navy pilots, who would never be replaced. The enemy could not recover and Guadalcanal, defended by a very tired band of pilots, was abandoned by the Japanese in February 1943.

In the meantime, the meager Allied Air Forces, Southwest Pacific Area (SWPA), were being revitalized under the command of Maj. Gen. George C. Kenney, a World War I fighter pilot with two kills, who had arrived in Australia in July 1942 to run Gen. Douglas MacArthur's Fifth Air Force. Understanding the limits of attrition warfare, Kenney allowed his subordinates to innovate with very little equipment. As Kenney was on his way from California, his first aide, 63rd Bomb Squadron commander Maj. William Benn, came up with the idea of low-level skip bombing to sink ships. Benn proved the concept in spades with six B-17s, which had consistently dismal results against moving ships from high altitude, and Kenney quickly put all his bomber crews, medium and heavy, on low-level skip-bombing missions.

Another of Kenney's innovators, Maj. Paul I. "Pappy" Gunn, got permission to install four forward-firing .50 caliber guns in the nose an A-20 Havoc. The results were so spectacular that Kenney ordered him to yank everything from the nose of a B-25 Mitchell, install as many .50s as possible, as well as two on each side and three beneath the fuselage, with a minimum of 500 rounds per gun. Even though only eight guns could be installed (four in the nose and four on the sides), Pappy lived up to his reputation. Kenney knew he had the ultimate "commerce destroyer" which could skip bomb and overwhelm deck defenses at the same time. Toward the end of 1942 and into early 1943, under Kenney's enthusiastic support, the 3rd Attack Group's Capt. Ed Larner, who was given command of the 90th Bomb Squadron, and Group CO Maj. John P. "Jock" Henebry developed the tactics for what became one of the deadliest weapons in the theater.

Kenney, always looking for what was available, ordered stockpiles of unused 23-pound parachute fragmentation ("parafrag") bombs from the States, then had them dropped on any and all targets possible. They turned enemy aircraft on the ground into scrap metal. He also utilized air transport to its full potential by resupplying even the most tenuous of Allied holds against the Japanese. By the end of 1942, in spite of dealing with an enemy superior in numbers with better performing aircraft, Kenney had complete control of the air over Papua, New Guinea...quite a feat considering the Bell P-39/P-400 Airacobra and Curtiss P-40 Warhawk were his primary fighters. In late 1942 the Seventh Air Force, to be centered on the Consolidated B-24 Liberator, began flying combat from the New Hebrides and, in January 1943, the Thirteenth Air Force was activated in the South Pacific under Maj. Gen. Nathan Twining. On January 22, 1943, the battle for Papua ended with the first decisive defeat of Japanese forces on land.

The arrival of the Lockheed P-38 Lightning in November 1942 gave the Army Air Forces in the Pacific their first

real dominance over Japanese fighters. Kenney had been lobbying Arnold strenuously for P-38s while Monk Hunter, VIII Fighter Command leader in the ETO, having lost his Lightnings to North Africa, did nothing to get replacement groups from the Z.I. (Zone of the Interior or the U.S.). Combined with Kenney's "commerce destroyers," all the '38 pilots needed was a chance to prove they could gain air superiority, thus freeing American attack aircraft to stop enemy convoys and invasion forces. That came with the Battle of the Bismarck Sea, March 2-4, 1943, as the enemy sought to bolster Lae, New Guinea, with a 16 ship convoy. Covered by P-38s, A-20s and B-25s modified with forward firing .50s entered combat for the first time. Joined by B-17s and Australian Beaufighters, the force sank, as best anyone

can figure, eight transport/cargop vessels and four destroyers, in the process killing over 3,000 men. For the first time a naval force had been destroyed by land-based air alone. Every medium bomber in the command was ordered to be modified and crews trained in low-level strike procedures.

The icing on the cake was the death of Isoroku Yamamoto on April 18, 1943. Intercepted by pilots of the 339th and 70th Fighter Squadrons, flying the only P-38s in the Solomons, Yamamoto went down with his Mitsubishi Betty bomber. Winning the war in the Pacific, at last, was viewed as a matter of time. Everyone knew it would be at terrible cost against a fierce enemy, but it *would* happen.

OPPOSITE: In the rays of a low sun on the late afternoon of August 8, 1942, a Navy Type 1 Attack Bomber, Mitsubishi G4M1...called Betty by the Allies...lies alongside the destroyer *Bagley* (DD-386) off Lunga near Guadalcanal, having lost its aft fuselage while ditching next to the ship. Out of 23 Type 1s from the IJN 5th Air Attack Force flying 560 miles one way from Rabaul, 17 went down to Wildcat fighters and withering antiaircraft fire from the American ships. Several of the enemy fighters, which flew escort out of Buin, 300 miles from Guadalcanal, were downed as well. It was the heaviest single loss of Japanese land attack aircraft during the long Guadalcanal campaign. As the *Bagley* neared this Betty, sailors on deck came under pistol fire from the Japanese crew sitting on the wing! Before much could be done the enemy fliers quickly committed suicide with their last rounds. Torpedo- and bomb-carrying G4M1s were effective long-range attackers with a maximum range of just over 3,700 miles without bomb load. On the down side, they lacked self-sealing fuel tanks and effective armor plate for crew protection. *National Archives*

ABOVE: Several Grumman F4F Wildcats, remnants of the "Cactus Air Force," sit at the edge of Henderson Field, Guadalcanal (Allied code name Cactus), in April 1943 awaiting repair or salvage. The battle for this piece of Solomon Islands real estate from August 7, 1942, through February 1943 resulted in the first successful U.S. offensive of the Pacific War. Needed by the Japanese to invade Port Moresby, the island airfield was the main objective and when it was taken it was held at all costs. The Americans had to have it to launch an effective air campaign to not only stop the Japanese but to hit their forward bases. When Brig. Gen. Roy S. Geiger took command of the pitifully small band of Navy and Marine aircraft flying from Henderson, he immediately went on the offensive. Marine pilots like Joe Bauer, John Smith, Bob Galer, Joe Foss and Marion Carl knew how to use the Wildcat to its advantages. In concert with Army P-39s and Navy aircraft "on loan" from their respective carriers, these tired, overworked, under-nourished men kept the Japanese from effectively using their air power and the 'Canal quickly became a base for offensive air operations. *National Archives*

LEFT: Lt. Charlie Wesley sits in his VF-11 Grumman F4F Wildcat at the fighter strip shared with the Marines east of Henderson Field, Guadalcanal, in the spring of 1943. The Sun Downers squadron insignia, painted below the windshield, was a clever depiction of two F4Fs punching holes in the Rising Sun, causing it to go down behind an ocean horizon. By the time VF-11 arrived at Cactus in late April for their first combat tour, *Saratoga* was in drydock for torpedo damage repair, *Wasp* had gone down, victim of a submarine's torpedo, and *Hornet* had been lost in the Battle of Santa Cruz. Only *Enterprise* was left. As a result, several Navy squadrons, including Fighting Eleven, were ordered to land-based duty, many co-based with the Marines on Guadalcanal. By this time the Marines had given up their Wildcats for new Corsairs and many Navy squadrons were transitioning to, or getting ready for, the new F6F-3 Hellcat. As a result, both VF-11 and VF-21 became the last two squadrons flying extensive combat in the old Grumman. There were plenty of them in the Fleet Aircraft Replacement Pool so getting transferred out of them in the theater was unlikely. In spite of potential morale problems, these pilots knew the strong points of their small fighter and used them well. In 11 weeks of combat, the Sun Downers were credited with 55 kills for the loss of 12 Wildcats in aerial combat, a kill-to-loss ratio of four-to-one. *Charles V. Wesley*

RIGHT: The history of the Boeing B-17 Flying Fortress in the Pacific was checkered at best. Although Billy Mitchell's demonstration of a bomber's ability to sink capital ships had been convincing, the reality of wartime proved very different. In order to make sure ships were hit, crews changed to skip bombing Of all B-17s flown out of the Philippines to Australia, only ten were close to being considered combat capable. Between December 1941 and March 1942, fifty-three new B-17Es left the U.S. for Australia and Java, but only 44 reached the 7th and 43rd Bomb Groups. Two months of combat brought that down to 19 with twelve Consolidated LB-30 Liberators filling out the ranks. Neither group managed to put up more than 10 Forts at a time out of Australia, at least until September when the 19th Bomb Group brought 45 newB-17Es like this one, with them and the 43rd was re-equipped with some new B-17Fs. The 19th transferred all of its Forts to the 43rd, making it, with 80 bombers, the sole Fifth Air Force B-17 unit. The 11th Bomb Group flew in the Central Pacific out of Midway during the battle for that famous island, then transferred to the Thirteenth Air Force in July 1942, flying out of New Caledonia, then Guadalcanal. By March 1943 the 11th went to the Seventh Air Force and made the transition to B-24 Liberators, the heavy bomber of choice in the Pacific. *Frederick H. Hill*

BELOW: Pilots of the 475th Fighter Group look over what's left of several Japanese Army Air Force Nakajima Ki-43-II Hayabusa (Peregrine Falcon) fighters at Hollandia, New Guinea, in May 1944. After entering production in March 1941, the Army's Ki-43 was quickly confused with the Navy's Zero by most Allied personnel. Lighter, more maneuverable and far simpler to build and maintain, the Hayabusa, code named Oscar, became the JAAF's most numerous fighter, committed to fighting on all fronts. Even though it could outmaneuver any opponent, the early Ki-43, like the Zero, did not have armor or self-sealing fuel tanks. Even worse, throughout the production run it had poor armament until the very last version appeared on the scene in late 1944, long after the line should have been shut down. All American pilots were warned not to dogfight with the Oscar or the Zero, particularly if the enemy pilot seemed to know what he was doing. The dive and slash attack, proven in battle by Chennault's Flying Tigers, worked very well. However, that didn't stop many from trying to twist and turn, one-on-one. Sometimes it worked, but the classic dogfight gave the Japanese winning cards if the pilot was experienced enough to play them. But he had to be very good indeed. If a blast of P-38 gunfire hit an Oscar, it was likely to be deskinned in seconds. *Dennis Glen Cooper*

BELOW: Several technicians try to figure out how to get this 67th Fighter Squadron Airacobra on its feet again after a belly landing in the tall grass of New Caledonia in 1942. This former French penal colony to the northeast of Australia was an ideal Allied staging base for aircraft being ferried or shipped into the theater. It quickly became known as one of the few rest and relaxation spots worth visiting on leave. In spite of its poor combat performance, the Bell P-39 (and its P-400 export version) and the P-40 were just about all there was in the Pacific to face those well-trained Japanese. The 8th and 35th Fighter Groups were sent to Australia in early 1942 with worn out P-39Ds. Most had around 1,000 hours flying time on them from stateside operations. The 8th was the first to take them into combat on April 30th after they were ferried from Australia to Port Moresby, a base desperately in need of fighter protection. Lt. Col. Buzz Wagner, who had become the AAF's first ace in the Philippines, led the 35th and 36th Fighter Squadrons on this strafing mission against the Japanese airfield at Lae, across the Owen Stanley Mountains on the east coast of New Guinea. *Barclay Dillon via Merle Olmsted*

ABOVE: After Pearl Harbor there was very real concern the Axis would hit the Panama Canal and block the flow of supplies to the Pacific. Though an attack never took place, several fighter and bomber groups were stationed in the Canal Zone with the Sixth Air Force. This Bell P-39Q Airacobra of the 53rd Fighter Group is getting some attention at Madden Field, Panama. Considered somewhat of a backwater, Panama, for the most part, did not get firstline aircraft off the assembly lines until 1944. Most pilots kept trying to transfer out to an active combat zone. Nevertheless, defense of the Canal was extremely important and many units were dedicated to sub hunting in both the Atlantic and the Pacific. Fighter pilots found great amusement in dogfighting with each other or watching native wildlife wander through their stilted huts at night. *USAF*

RIGHT: Another of the enemy aircraft left behind at Hollandia in May 1944 was this 10th Recon Sentai Mitsubishi Ki-51 Army Type 99, code named Sonia. The 10th's unit symbol on the tail represented the River Fuji. Looking very much like a scaled down version of its predecessor, the Ki-30 Ann, the Ki-51 was designed for the same "Assault Plane" light-bomber mission with the added ability to operate from short strips closer to the front. The aircraft was combat tested over China in 1940, where there was little effective opposition; then it was deployed with the JAAF across the Pacific. Despite a maximum speed of something like 260 mph, the Sonia was an effective tactical aircraft, easy to fly and maintain, very maneuverable and, thanks to some foresight, it had armor and self-sealing fuel tanks. Very much like the SBD, which was even slower! Production of the Army Type 99 continued through 1944 with a total run of 1,459. Although a tactical reconnaissance version was planned, Mitsubishi simply redesigned the rear seat for quick installation of cameras. As a result, mechanics in the field could adapt the Sonia to either mission, a real plus for ground commanders who needed both attack and reconnaissance aircraft on immediate notice. *Dennis Glen Cooper*

LEFT: When Allied attack aircraft swept across Japanese airfields, thanks to the small 23-pound parafrag bombs they really made mincemeat out of what was on the ground. The results are clearly evident on this Nakajima Ki-49-II Donryu (Storm Dragon), code named Helen, at Noemfoor Island, Netherlands East Indies, in June 1944. By this time in the war, the Helen was the most numerous of JAAF heavy bombers (in American vernacular, a medium bomber). Fortunately for its crews, the Army Type 100 Heavy Bomber Model 2A (Ki-49-IIa) had more powerful engines, increased armor protection, self-sealing fuel tanks and heavier defensive armament. The Ki-49 was also the first JAAF bomber with a tail gun position. On the downside, it was still too slow and was not as pleasant on the controls as the older Ki-21-II (Sally) it was supposed to replace. America's comparable bomber was the Douglas B-23, never committed to combat. Allied fighter pilots rarely found Japanese bombers of any type anything but meat on the table. The only thing they really had to watch when chasing the Helen was the 20mm cannon in the upper fuselage and 12.7mm machine gun in the tail. A high frontal attack was optimum. *Wilbur Kuhn via Inez Kuhn*

LEFT: Gary Cooper was clearly pleased with his first ride in a P-38 Lightning out of Dobodura, New Guinea, in late 1943. Stuffed in behind the pilot where the radios were normally installed, "piggy-back" style, he had been a part of the USO show visiting the 475th Fighter Group, the only P-38 unit to be created within a war zone rather than in the Z.I. Made up of a talented bunch of pilots and ground crews who had already seen a great deal of combat, the 475th – nicknamed Satan's Angels – went on to rack up one of the best combat records in the Pacific. Entertainers were more than welcome at these bases, which seemed to be at the hot, steaming end of the earth. Actress Una Merkel, among Cooper's troupe, was struck by how high morale seemed to be in spite of poor food, hot nights and malarial mosquitoes. Quite often the only relief a pilot could find was getting airborne, cooling off as altitude increased. There wasn't a Lightning pilot in the Pacific who didn't consider his fighter the best for the job. *Dennis Glen Cooper*

OPPOSITE: American markings went through some bewildering changes in 1943. On June 27th, the round national insignia had white rectangles added to either side, then a red surround was added to that. On September 17th, the red surround was changed to blue for fear of confusing it with the red Japanese Hinomaru insignia , though the red border often lasted into 1944 due to the press of wartime operations. This old Douglas B-18 (the 15th airframe built under the original contract) in Panama is an excellent example of that June 27th change order, which only lasted for three months. The tired bomber is probably attached to the 23rd Tow Target Squadron, a service unit for the 3rd Battalion, 508th Airborne Infantry, permanently garrisoned in the Canal Zone as a rapid deployment force in the event of invasion. The Panama Mobile Force, as it was called, was needed since nothing moved across the ground very fast with so much swamp and tropical overgrowth. The parachutes being loaded here are well equipped for an area with so much water (aircraft were never farther than 50 miles from the ocean in Panama). Chest and backpack chutes, Mae Wests and a survival kit for a seat cushion were standard issue. *USAF*

BELOW: Lt. Gen. George C. Kenney, commander of the Fifth Air Force, sits in the right seat of his personal stripped-down B-17E. In January 1941 Kenney was a lieutenant colonel but by March 1942 he had become a major general in charge of the Southwest stateside Fourth Air Force. When he was transferred to the Southwest Pacific as Gen. Douglas MacArthur's air commander, he proved he could get along with a very controversial boss by getting results. As MacArthur wrote after the war, "Through his extraordinary capacity to improvise and improve, he took a substandard force and welded it into a weapon so deadly as to take command of the air whenever it engaged the enemy." Kenney also cared for his men deeply, so much so they became known as "Kenney's Kids." Although saddled with third priority for aircraft behind Europe and the Navy, Kenney kept stinging the enemy with his low-level medium bombers and small numbers of fighters. In June 1944, the Fifth and Thirteenth Air Forces were combined into the Far East Air Forces (FEAF) under Kenney's command, a tribute to his ability to get the job done. *USAF*

RIGHT: Pacific airstrips were often crowded and pilots had to keep a wary eye out when entering the traffic pattern. Two aircraft, a Navy Douglas R4D and a fighter, burn at Vella Lavella after a midair collision over the field. Fortunately, the fighter pilot got out and is being cared for by the men near the jeep in the middle of the broad strip. Vella was a strategically important piece of real estate in the New Georgia group of the Solomon Islands. With an airfield on the western side of "The Slot," the strip of water which ran south of Bougainville toward Guadalcanal, the Allies could harass the Japanese, who quite effectively dominated nighttime naval operations in the area. North of the Solomons was New Britain and the enemy stronghold of Rabaul. Marine Corps pilots, in particular, flew from those strips nearest Rabaul, so Vella became critical to their success. Quite often, the terrible price paid did not directly involve getting shot at.
National Archives

BELOW: From the time it entered combat in late June 1943, flying out of Port Moresby, the 345th Bomb Group quickly established itself as one of the premier B-25 Mitchell low-level attack units in the Pacific. Eventually nicknamed the Air Apaches, the group personified the Fifth Air Force's ability to destroy just about anything it was assigned to attack. In the Southwest Pacific's war of attrition, every enemy installation or piece of equipment put out of action helped move the Allies closer to Japan and ending the war. The 500th Bomb Squadron's *Jock Juggler*, a Kansas City-built B-25D-25-NC (identical to the B-25C built in California), sits at Nadzab, New Guinea, in June 1944 in the middle of her combat career. After being assigned in March 1944 to the Rough Raiders, who painted the snorting horse on the tails of their Mitchells for six months in the middle of 1944, the aircraft was transferred to the 49th Service Group. The combat lives of most aircraft were short — new models came along, some were shot up, many got war weary. There wasn't a B-25 pilot in the Pacific who didn't think his aircraft was ideal for the mission.
George J. Fleury

OPPOSITE: When the 90th Bomb Group arrived at Iron Range, Australia, in November 1942, their new Consolidated B-24 Liberators were a sight to behold for battle weary U.S. Army Air Forces commanders who had been fighting the Japanese for almost a year with wornout aircraft. The 90th entered combat immediately, hitting enemy airfields, troops, ground installations and shipping in New Guinea. In February the unit moved to Port Moresby, New Guinea, just in time to participate in the Battle of the Bismarck Sea in early March 1943. With the Group's excellent record of "piracy" against enemy shipping on the high seas and 90th commanding officer Col. Art Rogers at the helm, the unit got its nickname, The Jolly Rogers, from Lt. Bernard Stoecklein, a born promoter. The Liberator's massive twin vertical stabilizers were ideal for flying the Jolly Roger flag, so Sgt. Leonard Baer painted the first skull and cross bombs on the tail of Rogers' B-24D, *Connell's Special*, in time for the Wewak, New Guinea mission of August 18, 1943. Rogers had dedicated the ship to Brig. Gen. Carl Connell, who ran Air Service Command in Brisbane and was responsible for putting a tail turret in the nose. In no time every 90th aircraft had the grinning apparition painted on its tails. The tradition was carried on with *Connell's Special The 2nd*, seen here at Biak, New Guinea, in 1944. *Glenn R. Horton, Jr.*

RIGHT: A Grumman F6F-3 Hellcat of VF-1 runs up in the chocks prior to launch from the newly commissioned USS *Yorktown* (CV-10) in the spring of 1943. Though the new tricolor paint scheme and removal of the lower-left/upper-right national insignia on the wings had been authorized the previous February, this fighter has not been repainted. Who had time? Most mechanics were incredulous at what they considered to be a steady stream of whimsical markings or paint changes when there was a war to fight. No sooner would one directive come out than another took its place. If one waited long enough, he could avoid most of the effort since it was going to disappear anyway. When *Yorktown*-based VF-5 took the Hellcat into combat for the first time in August 1943, the different colored splotches of paint and covered-over markings made them look battle weary from the start. The Hellcat and the Vought F4U Corsair, both of which entered service in early 1943, brought about a drastic change in the naval fighter war over the Pacific. These two tough, heavily armed and powerful fighters eliminated the Zero's dominance immediately, enabling American carriers to hunt the enemy with deadly effectiveness. *National Archives*

LEFT: The 58th Fighter Group flew P-47 Thunderbolts during its entire combat tour with the Fifth Air Force, from February 1944 to the surrender. With the aircraft's ideal large cowling for his "canvas," 58th nose artist Cpl. Jack B. Wallace quickly became known as one of the more talented practitioners of the genre in the Pacific. His work on the 310th Fighter Squadron's *Pioneer Peggy* was a striking example of what pilots were more than pleased to carry into combat on their P-47s. After flying Curtiss P-40L Warhawks off the USS *Ranger* in February 1943 as replacements for units in North Africa, the 58th completed transition to P-47s in the U.S. They shipped out to New Guinea for duty primarily as a ground attack outfit. Gen. Kenney considered the Douglas A-24s (Army SBD Dauntlesses) previously supplied to be virtually useless cannon fodder. Once believed too large and ungainly for doing battle with nimble Japanese fighters, the T-bolt quickly earned a reputation as a deadly weapon. In August 1944 the group moved to Noemfoor, Netherlands East Indies, then to the Philippines in November. After strafing a Japanese naval force into junk off Mindoro on December 26, 1944, the 58th was awarded a Distinguished Unit Citation for preventing the destruction of the American base on the island. *George E. Miltz, Jr.*

OPPOSITE: With a thumbs up from the plane captain that everything is set for launch, a VF-5 Grumman F6F-3 Hellcat is about to be waved off the USS *Yorktown* on a strike in late 1943. Most pilots considered the Hellcat ideal for combat in the Pacific. Not only was it one of the easiest aircraft to bring aboard ship, controllable even when in a full stall, it was effortless to manage in combat with simple systems and six excellent .50 caliber Browning machine guns. As in all the aircraft it powered, the Pratt & Whitney R-2800 Double Wasp engine could be shot to pieces and still produce enough power to bring pilot and aircraft home. Leading Navy ace David McCampbell, who got all of his 34 kills in the Hellcat, recalls watching the connecting rods pop in and out of the top of his damaged engine when coming back to the ship after being hit. Certainly it ran rough and was throwing oil, but it still got him back on the deck. *National Archives*

LEFT: Lined up for take-off on the strip at Green Island, north of Bougainville, Solomon Islands, May 1944, these two Douglas SBD-5 Dauntlesses of Marine Air Group 14 were ready to hit the Japanese bastion of Rabaul, 115 miles away. Along with their Navy and AAF counterparts, the Marines did their part in eliminating Rabaul, a natural harbor on the northeast tip of New Britain, without an invasion, saving countless lives in the process. This campaign was an excellent example of what air power could do, particularly when the services coordinated their efforts. While the SBD was considered obsolete even before the war started, it was never replaced by a more effective dive/scout-bomber for its mission during the conflict, unless one includes fighter-bombers like the F6F, F4U and P-47. In spite of having some excellent aircraft, Marines were used to taking hand-me-downs and making do as best they could. Close air support quickly became their specialty...USMC pilots were known for pressing in very close to make sure friendly troops on the ground weren't overrun by the enemy. *National Archives*

RIGHT: A captured Mitsubishi A6M Zero sits at Morotai, Halmahera Islands, to the northwest of New Guinea, ready for an evaluation flight under the joint Allied Technical Air Intelligence Unit (TAIU). Formed at Melbourne, Australia, as a loose, ad hoc organization in early 1943, the TAIU was tasked with finding anything and everything connected with Japanese aviation, from documents to entire aircraft. The British forces were very much a part of the effort, as can be seen by the rough approximation of the Royal Navy insignia on the side of this aircraft. One of the most difficult jobs faced by the TAIU personnel wasn't finding an aircraft, but keeping it cordoned off from eager GIs. As aviation historian Robert K. Mikesh has reported, the Unit's intelligence gatherers often said, "The Germans fought for Hitler, the Japanese fought for their Emperor, and the Americans fought for souvenirs." It was not unusual to find a perfectly good Japanese aircraft sitting on its wheels, ready to go, with the skin carrying national markings hacked out of the wings and fuselage by a hatchet or some other crude bludgeon. *Donald A. Soderlund, Jr.*

ABOVE: 1st Lt. Robert W. McClurg rests in his F4U Corsair after a raid on Rabaul in May 1944. During the last part of 1943, McClurg racked up seven kills with VMF-214, better known as Pappy Boyington's Black Sheep – an effective user of the F4U with 127 kills gained in only a few months of combat during late 1943. McClurg was one of Pappy's favorite wingmen and, as were most of the squadron's pilots, a real good "stick" and devotee of the Corsair. Boyington took command of 214 at Munda on September 7, 1943, when it was reorganized, quickly putting his special brand of free-wheeling fighter tactics on the unit. In October the squadron went back to Espiritu Santo, where it had first worked up in February 1943 with veterans of Midway as a nucleus. In late November Pappy took his men to Vella Lavella and 214 made its first fighter sweep against Rabaul on December 17th. On January 3, 1944, Boyington was lost in action (he became a POW) and the Black Sheep were withdrawn from combat, then sent back to the U.S. for carrier training. Assigned to the USS *Franklin*, the Black Sheep flew their initial second tour combat mission on March 18, 1945. The next day the ship was almost destroyed by enemy air attack, ending VMF-214's part in World War II. *National Archives*

OPPOSITE: The F4U-1 Corsairs of VMF-222 stand ready at Vella Lavella Island on December 15, 1943. Two days later the squadron took part in the first Marine Corps fighter sweep over Rabaul. The Flying Deuces, like so many other Marine Corsair squadrons, were gypsies who hopped from one scraped-out Pacific airstrip to another as the war moved up the island chains toward Japan. At Vella from November 1943 to January 1944 under Maj. Alfred Gordon, 222 was co-based on the strip with Maj. Marion Carl's VMF-223. The taking of Vella Lavella on August 15, 1943, was the first island-hopping bypass operation of the Pacific War, except for the North Pacific jump over Kiska in the Aleutians when Attu was invaded on May 11, 1943. Typical of his style, the hop over Kolombangara, with its 10,000 Japanese troops, had been proposed by Adm. Bill Halsey to Nimitz, who thought it was a great idea. Halsey and Nimitz made a real pair, two aggressive, risk-taking commanders who knew, by instinct, the difference between recklessness and daring. Their Japanese counterparts, on the other hand, showed a puzzling combination of needless caution, often losing the initiative, and reckless, last ditch engagements which were fought with frightening fanaticism to the last man for no gain. *National Archives via Jim Sullivan*

RIGHT: Marine Corps Sgt. P.J. Weber, chief engineer, shows co-pilot Capt. Campbell a map of New Georgia while flying their Consolidated PB4Y-1 Liberator out of Guadalcanal in December 1942. A Navy version of the B-24, the PB4Y was developed as a land-based alternative to flying boat patrol bombers. The Royal Air Force had already been flying Liberators in combat with Coastal Command, hunting for enemy shipping and submarines, with great results. The first B-24Ds pulled off the line as PB4Y-1s reached Navy squadrons in August 1942. As the AAF would later find out, the Liberator was ideal for the long overwater flights required in the Pacific. Well armed and armored, the four-engine bomber not only harassed enemy shipping, but flew long range reconnaissance from many island bases. Marine crews were assigned to PB4Ys to fly alongside their Navy counterparts, although there was little differentiation as to who was doing what for whom. In the early stages of the war, interservice rivalry meant far less than simple survival. *National Archives*

ABOVE: The boneyard at Torokina on Bougainville was quite a sight in 1944. The Corsair was tossed aside by VMF-214, the Black Sheep, while the P-39 Airacobra was left behind by the 70th Fighter Squadron. The 70th, attached to the Thirteenth Air Force's 18th Fighter Group, had moved up through Fiji to Guadalcanal and the other islands in the Solomon chain. With spare parts in such limited supply at the ends of the long Pacific logistics pipeline, salvaged aircraft became quite valuable to mechanics who had to keep their other charges airworthy. These two markedly different fighters operated together quite often, with the '39s flying low, below 15,000 feet, and the Corsairs high, around 25,000 feet. In spite of some strong interservice rivalry at the command level, when American pilots were on the same strip they didn't care much about their differences, except for the good-natured ribbing common to all combat pilots. The 'Cobras would often take on the ground targets, which they did quite effectively, with the Corsairs flying top cover. This also made the Army fighters bait for enemy fighters...not much fun for a '39 pilot but a great opportunity for the Marines if the Japanese took the lure. *National Archives via Jim Sullivan*

ABOVE: The bare, forbidding landscape of the Aleutian Islands was well represented by Cold Bay, where this 77th Bomb Squadron Martin B-26-MA Marauder was temporarily based in October 1942. The pyramidal tents on the left were considered standard living quarters while the huts on the right usually served as operations...or a poor man's officer's club. Transferred to Alaska in late December 1941, long before the Japanese invasion a half-year later in June, the 77th flew some of the first production Marauders in combat, quickly learning both the strong and the weak points of the sleek medium bomber. By far the most daunting task was keeping the aircraft operational in the miserable weather. The damp cold seemed to penetrate not only flesh but the most carefully sealed ignition harnesses and magnetos. The moist air would often condense and freeze in the tops of several spark plugs, causing the porcelain cigarette-shaped harness leads to crack. This shorted out ignition spark to the plug, in turn causing power-robbing misfire in the engine. A simple enough problem to fix, but with 18 cylinders to check, and two plugs in each cylinder, that meant taking the cowling off, then pulling and checking 36 leads with bare hands (dangerous) in the numbing outdoors. *Robert Blair*

ABOVE: The first Lockheed Lightnings to go into action as fighters (photo recon F-4s were the first of the type to enter combat in May 1942 in the Pacific) were early production P-38Es assigned to the Aleutians-based 54th Fighter Squadron in August 1942. Although modified to early F model standards, these Es were still not quite what the doctor ordered. Nevertheless, the 54th's pilots were very happy to have them, particularly when compared with the P-39s and P-40s that were standard equipment for the war in the Arctic. These men have just finished a briefing and are walking out to their Lightnings in late 1942 at Adak. The second (No.76) in line, *Itsy Bitsy*, was flown by Capt. George Laven, who got two kills in theater and would later go on to fly Lightnings in the Southwest Pacific with the 49th Fighter Group. The mud, which pierced-steel plank could not stop, was a continual menace to operations. Finding enough warm clothing was also a major concern since the P-38 never had adequate cockpit heat. Those pilots were cold whether they were flying or not. *National Archives*

OPPOSITE: Lockheed P-38 Lightnings were the first true multimission fighters, able to perform a variety of tasks quite effectively. These ground crewmen hang what appears to be a 1,000-pound bomb on the left underwing shackle using the standard field kit manual hoists which were built to use the shackle itself as a hoist point. A thousand pounder was actually lighter than a standard filled 165-gallon drop tank and about half the weight of a full 310-gallon drop tank. Early P-38Es and Fs could carry at least 2,000 pounds of bombs or fuel tanks externally, later upped to 4,000 pounds. As an excellent dive- and level-bomber with effortless aiming of the four .50 calibers and one 20mm cannon, the '38 was used extensively in the ground attack role in all theaters. In the last year of the Pacific War, P-38s dropped a new substance called napalm, essentially jellied gasoline and quite a deadly firebomb. Basically, the Lightning could carry or drop just about anything hung on it. With twin-engine hauling power and an efficient high-lift wing, the Kelly Johnson design had so much growth potential it became a much sought-after weapon of war, particularly by George Kenney who firmly believed it was the ideal fighter for the Pacific Theater. *National Archives*

RIGHT: Capt. Morgan A. Giffin, 54th Fighter Squadron, stands next to his P-38E at Adak, Aleutian Islands, in late 1942. His A-2 jacket carries a leather patch of the squadron insignia, a leopard with white boxing gloves intercepting and destroying an enemy bomb. This emblem was also carried on the outer Prestone radiator housings of each boom. His helmet has had separate headphones – normally worn on a bare head or over a hat – grafted into the ear pieces, possibly because that was all there was available in the way of reliable equipment. On February 13, 1943, Giffin was credited with shooting down an Aichi E13A reconnaissance seaplane, code named Jake. Of the fighter units in the Aleutians, the 54th Squadron was by far the most successful with at least 14 of the 34 confirmed kills in the campaign, which made the P-38 the most effective fighter as well. The tobacco stains on Giffin's fingers were normal for World War II when smoking was considered standard recreation and a "tribal" custom. The fighter pilot's apocryphal breakfast of coffee and cigarettes was not all that far off, particularly in the rushed atmosphere of a combat unit. *National Archives*

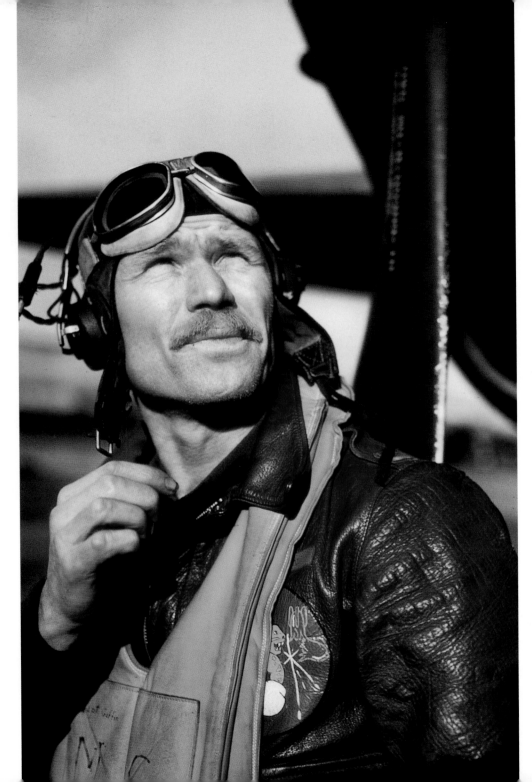

ABOVE: A Fleet Air Wing 4 Consolidated PBY-5A Catalina, with four Mark 37 depth charges hung under the wings, is ready for a mission, January 11, 1943, in the Aleutians. The venerable flying boat, first ordered in 1933, was another anachronism which, against the odds, proved quite effective in wartime more than a decade later. The PBY-5A amphibian development was the most useful of the series, able to operate from shore and sea, and with a range of over 2,000 miles it could hunt down enemy submarines and shipping quite effectively. The total underwing external load could be pushed to 4,000 pounds of bombs, two 2,200-pound Mark XIII torpedoes or four 325-pound depth charges. The Cat was ideal for the constant poor weather in the theater, with standard ceilings of 500 to zero feet, accompanied by constant rain and fog. Crews aboard PBYs and Army OA-10s made low flying an art to stay out of the clouds, often brushing the waves. One PBY crew in the Aleutians found itself completely lost at night in heavy fog and rain. They headed out toward what they calculated was open sea, gradually let down until contacting the water, settled to a stop, then turned around and taxied back to shore until the weather lifted. Few wartime aircraft could perform such a feat. *National Archives*

OPPOSITE: World War II was an adventure in camouflage variation in all services, surface or air. The Navy's stream of directive changes, in both camouflage and markings, was often confusing but, on the whole, the results were quite effective. This Grumman Goose – most likely a rare JRF-1A – is an excellent example of what Non-specular Blue Grey and Light Grey could do over the Alaskan terrain in 1942. Ordered by the Navy as utility transports, the first civil Grumman G-21s came off the line as JRF-1s in late 1939 with a few set aside for target-towing and photography. The JRF-4 was modified to carry two 250-pound bombs or depth charges under the wings and, in 1941, the primary production version was created, the -5 with uprated Pratt & Whitney R-985 engines and cameras for aerial survey. The Goose was quite a versatile utility aircraft for doing any number of small jobs, from moving personnel to attacking a submarine, because it was an amphibian, able to land on water or a shore base. *National Archives*

BELOW: Moored in Massacre Bay, Attu, Aleutians, three motor torpedo boats (MTBs) and a PBY Catalina take on fuel from the seaplane tender USS *Gillis* on June 21, 1943. PT boats were never far from a fixed aviation facility or a tender since the three Packard V-12s in each boat required lots of high-octane aviation fuel. From the first Aleutian engagements in early June 1942, the *Gillis* was a fighting ship in every sense of the word, serving as a forward base to launch its PBYs time and again against the enemy fleet and shore bases. With a large store of bombs, ammunition and fuel, her Cats, particularly those from patrol squadrons VP-41, VP-43 and VP-51, accounted for several ships sunk and she always seemed to be in just the right place to harass the Japanese, even in the worst weather. The PBY/tender combination was an ideal platform for round-the-clock bombing, which was first tried against Kiska. The Japanese were incredulous, reporting an attack by giant dive-bombers which looked like patrol planes. Unfortunately, such intense action in these vulnerable boats resulted in 10 of the 20 Catalinas being destroyed or damaged during the "Kiska Blitz." From June 14th on the PBYs resorted to their normal routine of long-range patrol, enemy ship hunting and rescue. *National Archives*

Catalinas and Venturas of Fleet Air Wing 4 squat at readiness in the Aleutians on December 16, 1943, a very good weather day indeed. Both aircraft, though radically different, complemented each other quite well in performing the same mission of long-range patrol and bombing. The PBY-5A, with something like 24 hours of fuel aboard, could range far out into the ocean in search of prey. Quite often, "Cat" crews, rather than try and sink what they found, would radio position reports back to shore and the high-speed PV-1s would head out for the attack. As in every other theater in which they flew, PBY units became very skilled at air-sea rescue. Navy patrol-bomber crews, regardless of what they were flying, became quite adept at their jobs by this time in the war. Since the conflict in the Aleutians was over by mid-August 1943, due as much to the weather as anything else, those PBYs left in the theater were doomed to one long-range, boring patrol after another, with only an air-sea rescue mission every now and then, looking for nonexistent enemy shipping. The winds were often so strong an outbound leg would take two hours while the trip back would last eight hours. *National Archives*

ABOVE: This 11th Fighter Squadron, 343rd Fighter Group, revetment at Adak, full of Curtiss P-40 Warhawks, is dry for a change on a clear autumn 1943 day. What would have been mud is now a fine silt, which seemed to get into everything when engines were started. Commanded in the early actions (September to November 1942) by Lt. Col. John S. "Jack" Chennault, son of Gen. Claire Chennault, the 343rd carried Bengal Tiger faces on the noses of many of its P-40s, though the 11th Squadron was the real proponent, becoming known as the Aleutian Tigers. Next to the runway a 28th Composite Group B-24 sits ready to go. With so little cockpit heat, the P-40 was miserable to fly in the damp cold of the Aleutians. For that matter, almost all World War II aircraft had minuscule sources of heat for their crews. With the penetrating drizzle which always seemed common in this theater of war, crews suffered a continual lack ability to get warm, from poorly insulated sleeping bags and leaky pyramidal tents to drafty cockpits. *National Archives*

OPPOSITE: Even on a clear day, the 343rd Fighter Group line at Amchitka didn't look all that inviting in 1944, but at least the pilots got to fly. The ground crews had nothing that exciting to break the boredom. After awhile, pilots were scrambled to intercept anything that moved. Glen Ellis remembers greeting every Liberty ship, C-47 transport, whale and sea lion that made a blip on the radar screen. The group commander thought every pilot, regardless of affiliation, should fly every type in the theater. Accordingly, Northwest Airlines pilots were checked out in P-40s and P-40 pilots were checked out in DC-3s. As could be expected, the airline boys always seemed to have some frozen milk or other scarce commodity, to bring back to the base. By this time, the Bengal Tiger markings were, for the most part, gone, being too much trouble to paint and maintain in the cold. Whenever replacement cowlings were fitted to the Warhawks, it wasn't unusual to see half a tiger on many aircraft. After Chennault left the 343rd in November 1942, the group was commanded by some other well know AAF pilots, including Lt. Col. Anthony V. Grossetta and Lt. Col. Dean Davenport, the co-pilot of Ted Lawson's B-25B on the Doolittle Tokyo Raid. *Glen R. Ellis*

LEFT: Standing in the chill with his P-40 Warhawk at Amchitka in 1944, this 18th Fighter Squadron, 343rd Fighter Group, pilot almost manages a smile. By this time the active war had already left the Aleutians. Fighter pilots were assigned defensive patrol up and down a very long chain of bleak islands with boredom the main enemy. Most thought the Japanese wouldn't be crazy enough to come back, but that was not a good enough reason to stand down defensive fighter cover. This certainly wasn't a cause for celebration among 18th Squadron pilots, who lived in tents pitched on the side of the hill adjacent to the flight line. When the weather went sour (most of the time), they sat huddled inside with nothing to do but shiver. Many pilots, after continual requests, managed to gets transferred out to an active combat zone or stateside duty. *Glen R. Ellis*

OPPOSITE: The first American Lockheed-Vega PV-1 Ventura squadrons to go into combat, VB-135 and -136, headed for the Aleutians, arriving at Adak in April 1943. With an onboard search radar, Venturas were put to work as pathfinders for Eleventh Air Force B-24s attacking Kiska. Navy VB-135 quickly developed effective radar bombing techniques which, to some degree, overcame the drastic Aleutian weather. After proving itself on several successful missions, the fast, maneuverable PV became one of the most useful weapons in the theater. These aviation ordnancemen are loading 500-pound bombs on the squadron flight line at Attu in late summer 1943, just before additional Ventura squadrons arrived to take the war to the Kuriles and Shimushu, the closest enemy bastions at the northern end of the Japanese islands. Night bombing and photography were added to the list of the aircraft's missions, which often lasted nine or ten hours. After coming home in December 1943 with VB-135 and -136 for refit and relaxation, Lt. Cdr. W.R. Stevens told Lockheed personnel the PV-1 was "a plenty sweet ship and will do anything. She maneuvers like a fighter, and we flew her through fog and weather so thick you could butter bread with it." *National Archives*

ABOVE: A beaching crew gets ready to take a Vought-Sikorsky OS2U-3 Kingfisher down the ramp into the frigid Aleutian water in mid 1943. Navy scout crews had their own boring tasks to cope with at this point in a theater without an active enemy. The Japanese made a point of staying away after leaving the previous August, having had their fill of terrible living conditions and the near impossibility of winning a war in the Arctic. Kingfishers were relegated to the mission everyone else seemed to have, cruising around on ceaseless patrol. Fortunately the aircraft was also an excellent air-sea rescue asset, particularly for fighter pilots since it could rarely pick up more than one person and get back off the water. Like the Catalina, it could also be flown right down to the wavetops without the danger of going in, unless the pilot got careless and stuck the nose of that main float into the water at too steep an angle. In spite of being an antique, in both design and mission, the OS2U continued to fly as a first-line aircraft until the war ended, when it rapidly disappeared. *National Archives*

ABOVE: The VB-136 Lockheed-Vega PV-1 Ventura of John McLennan squats on snow-covered Attu in June 1944, ready for the next mission. The squadron had just arrived after refit for its second Aleutian tour. At this point in the war, Navy Venturas were flying 700 nautical miles to the Kuriles and back to hit shipping and land targets on Paramushire and Shimushu. Japanese fear of an American invasion resulted in an increasing enemy fighter umbrella, giving PV crews a taste of the real war. Flying without fighter escort, Venturas often shot down enemy fighters, both with forward firing guns like another fighter and with the upper turret. If that didn't work, they outran them! Most of the time the patrol bombers would fly under 2,000 feet, looking for Japanese picket ships 200 miles out from the Kuriles. When attacking land targets they would go down to "zero" feet at wavetop height to avoid getting picked up on radar. Ground attack became a new mission when VB-136 and VPB-131 got PV-1s with 5" HVAR rockets and five forward firing .50s. The bomb bay was fitted with an additional 480 gallons of fuel, giving these bombers a real punch, but not without cost. Ten aircraft were lost by -135 while -136 lost six crews out of eighteen. Many made emergency diversions to Petropavalosk, on the Kamchatka peninsula in Russia, only seven miles from the Kuriles, but that often meant being interned for the duration. Some crews got out through Iran via Vladivostok. *John E. McLennan*

Grumman F4F-4 Wildcat BuNo. 03914 was flown by Lt. Bill Rawie in Fighting Six (VF-6) off the USS *Enterprise* (CV-6) in these unorthodox markings, February 1942. It carried nine red and white tail stripes (instead of 13) and unusually small red discs on the fuselage national insignia, left and right sides.

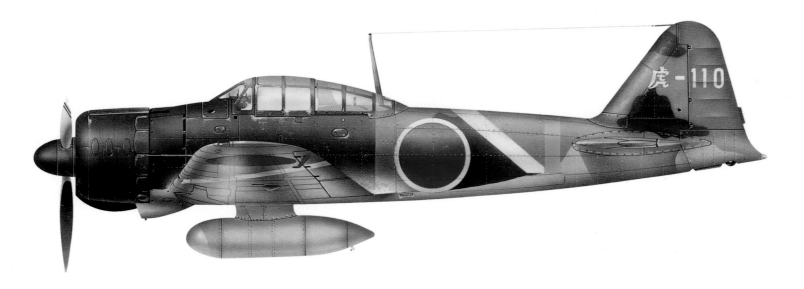

88   Mitsubishi A6M2b Model 21 Type 0 (Reisen) Navy carrier fighter "Tiger 110" was the 261st Naval Air Group commander's aircraft. The unusual paint scheme resulted from the need to operate from land bases after excessive carrier losses.

Bell's Airacobra I in RAF service was Over Sold, Over There and Overwhelmed, resulting in it being withdrawn from combat against the Luftwaffe. Absorbed by the USAAF as the P-400, it could barely fight off 308 mph JAAF Hayabusas. The 8th Fighter Group's No.19 was flown by 80th Squadron pilot Lt. Norb Ruff out of New Guinea.

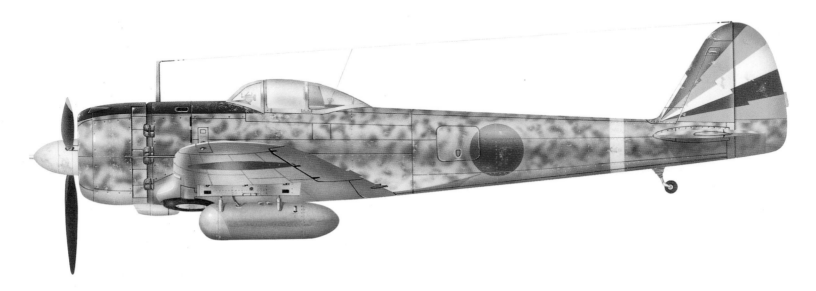

Nakajima Ki-43-IIb Hayabusa (Peregrine Falcon), assigned to the 11th Fighter Sentai, was the commander's aircraft in the Dutch East Indies, 1942. The vertical surfaces were marked with the color of each Chutai within the Sentai—the 1st, 2nd and 3rd Chutai colors were white, red and yellow respectively.

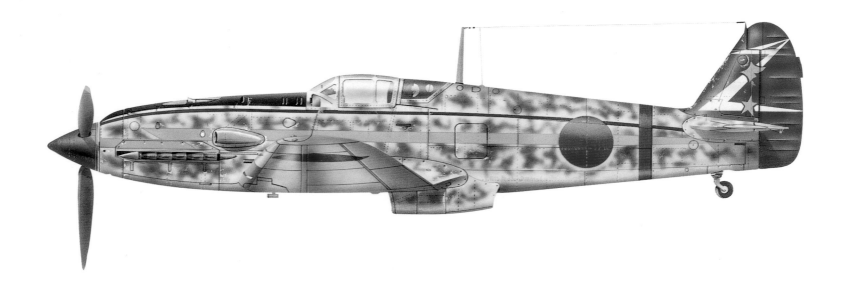

Kawasaki Ki-61-I Hien (Swallow) home defense fighter, assigned to the 224th Air Combat Regiment, Headquarters Company, in the Shinten (Heavens Shaking) Air Superiority Unit. The special color scheme was intended for home islands publicity. Japan's only inline liquid-cooled engine fighter, the Hien was designed in the same time frame as the P-51 Mustang.

Curtiss Kittyhawk Mk.IV *Hot Stuff* with No.78 Squadron, Royal Australian Air Force, was based at Noemfoor, Dutch New Guinea. Thousands of the Curtiss Hawk series fought across the globe in World War II, although a 1935 airframe mated to a good low altitude engine was not the ideal formula in most wartime skies.

Republic P-47D-15-RA Thunderbolts, unlike German, Japanese, Italian and Russian fighters, had to fight – and win – on just about every front in the world. *Marge - A Minnesota Maid*, AC42-23213, belonged to the 69th Squadron, 58th Fighter Group in late 1944 on Mindoro Island, P.I.

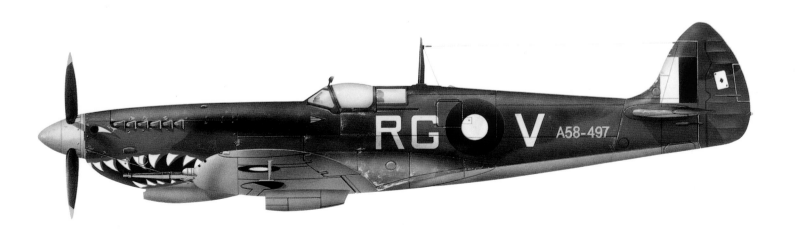

Vickers-Supermarine Spitfire LF.VIII, Royal Australian Air Force, based at Sattler Field, Northern Territory, in July 1944. Normally flown by Wing Cdr. Robert Gibbes, credited with 10 confirmed victories and five probables, the Spit was written off in a landing accident while being flown by another pilot in December 1944.

Chance Vought F4U-1D Corsair with VMF-324, the Day's Knights, Second Marine Air Wing, at Kadena, Okinawa, in April 1945. The USMC aircraft of choice, the Corsair was a magnificent and courageous leap forward when first flown in 1940. The P&W R-2800 engine was even better, just when needed most.

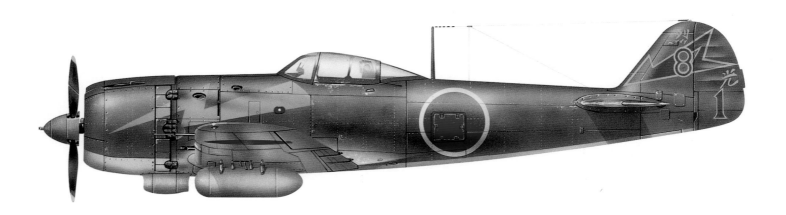

Nakajima Ki-84-Ia Hayate (Gale) with a standard 7,500 pounds takeoff gross weight, outperformed the P-51D-25 and P-47D-35 at the 20,000 foot critical altitude in tests with a captured aircraft. Perhaps, but both U.S. fighters were tougher, longer ranging and were best at 30,000 feet.

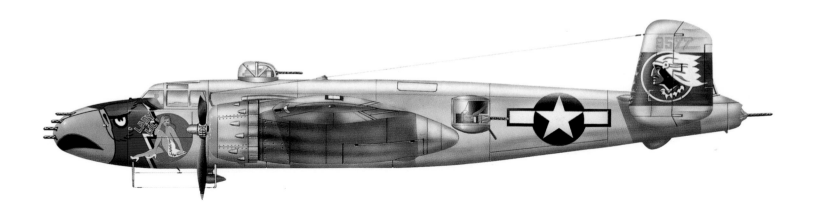

North American B-25J-22-NC Mitchell *Lady Lil*, AC44-29577, was a workhorse with the 498th Squadron, 345th Bomb Group Air Apaches out of Clark Field, P.I., in 1945. This colorful strafer, with a scythe of twelve .50 caliber forward firing Brownings, evolved from the original Mitchell medium bomber in the SWPA.

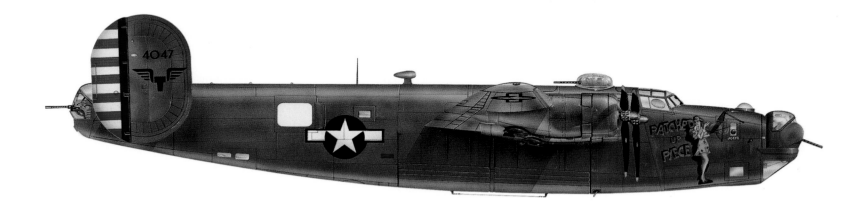

Consolidated F-7A Liberator *Patched Up Piece*, AC42-64047, was built as the first B-24J-1-CF. Converted to photo-recon duties, it was flown by John Wooten , Larry Thibault and David Ecoff with the 20th Combat Mapping Squadron in New Guinea. She was the first in a long line of exeptional nose art creations by Cpl. Al Merkling. The blue Synthetic Haze Paint was later stripped off...but the nose art remained.

3 OVER THE HUMP

CHINA-BURMA-INDIA

The Japanese had been at war with the Chinese long before the attack on Pearl Harbor, specifically since September 1931 with the conquest of Manchuria in northeastern China. In July 1937, the same month Amelia Earhart disappeared, the Japanese – after pouring troops into China's five northern provinces – struck near Peking, shelled Shanghai and began bombing several cities. President Roosevelt wanted to "quarantine the aggressors" with the help of other nations. The isolationists, led by the America First Committee, had a different agenda and prevented him from gaining much public support.

By the end of 1937 the Japanese captured Nanking, Chiang Kai-shek's capital, slaughtering more than 50,000 civilians with over 20,000 documented cases of rape. Even though this seemed to shake Americans out of their lethargy, they didn't want to hear the war warnings. Something like 2,500,000 Chinese had been killed by 1939 and Japan proclaimed the conquered nation a foundation of the Greater East Asia Co-Prosperity Sphere.

The only effective help from America for the beleaguered Chinese came from a partially deaf retired Army Air Corps captain named Claire L. Chennault. A fighter gadfly among bomber true believers at the Air Corps Tactical School in the mid 1930s, Chennault refused to believe bombers could not be shot down by fighters. After he retired in 1937, the Chinese offered him the job of training their fighter pilots. The odds didn't seem to phase him at all. By 1941 he was back in the U.S. recruiting pilots and ground crews for the 1st American Volunteer Group to fight the Japanese as an independent force. They would be flying Hawk 81s – basically equal to Army Air Corps P-40Cs – originally earmarked for the Royal Air Force. Even though there were 84 pilots ready for action by November, the AVG's first combat did not take place until December 20th, two weeks after the attack on Pearl Harbor. For six months this small band, better known as the Flying Tigers, were one of the few effective American forces opposing a wildly victorious enemy, claiming 286 enemy aircraft shot down for the loss of eight volunteer pilots killed, another four missing in action, and three killed on the ground.

The AVG, however, could only do so much. Not only were they a small force to begin with, but Chennault never got his 2nd AVG fighter outfit or his bomber group. Sadly, he was never informed of the Doolittle Raid in April so he was unable to prepare fields for recovery of the aircraft, which were all lost. The B-25s

OPPOSITE: The clash of cultures in the CBI was a wonder to both the Americans and the Chinese, clearly evident as this family walks past a 491st Squadron, 341st Bomb Group North American B-25C or D Mitchell at Yangkai, China, in the spring of 1945. Carrying most of the offensive load in the theater, the B-25 was certainly the workhorse bomber of the CBI, just as the P-40 was the workhorse fighter. Easy to fly and maintain, it seemed to be about all things to all people, from interdiction to bridge and railroad busting. The Ringer Squadron, as the 491st was known, had a history dating back to combat in World War I. Arriving in Karachi in September 1942, they flew out of Chakulia, India, with the Tenth Air Force for most of 1943, then moved on to Yangkai and the Fourteenth Air Force in January 1944. Typical of most CBI squadrons, detachments were broken off for operations out of Kweilin and Liuchow in the summer and fall of 1944. Seldom was the entire squadron, much less the whole 341st Bomb Group, in one spot at any one time. This didn't do much for squadron commanders but it certainly spread the assets around where most needed. *Carroll S. Barnwell*

would have formed the basis of his bomber unit. As a result, at any one time there were seldom more than a handful of combat ready aircraft on the line. The Japanese held most of China and conquered, essentially, all of Burma. Only India, in what became the China-Burma-India (CBI) Theater of Operations, remained free, and the enemy looked as if it was going to get that as well.

In April 1942, Chennault was recalled to active duty, promoted to brigadier general and given command of all AAF units in China, consolidated under the China Air Task Force, which would become the Fourteenth Air Force by March 1943. On July 4, 1942, the AVG disbanded. The remnants formed the basis of the 23rd Fighter Group, commanded by Col. Robert L. Scott, an AAF pilot who had managed to fly several missions with the AVG as an observer. Replacement P-40Es and B-25s were flown in from India but it would take some time to get a realistic operational capability in place. Since the Japanese controlled the Burma Road, the only way to resupply those units in China as by air, over the Himalayan Mountains. As a result, the first airlift in history was created in April 1942 to fly "the Hump" with every transport plane the Army could muster. This later grew into the Air Transport Command's shining hour, keeping China and those fighting there in the war.

In India, the Tenth Air Force was created under Maj. Gen. Lewis H. Brereton from the remnants of his Far East Air Forces which had evacuated the Philippines. There really wasn't a great deal left to fight with until March 1942 when the 7th Bomb Group, with B-17Es, and the 51st Fighter Group, with P-40Es, arrived at Karachi. Unfortunately there still weren't enough aircraft to make much of a difference. Between the pin pricks from the CATF in China and the Tenth Air Force in India, the Japanese were little more than irritated through most of 1942. By early 1943 some very real striking power was beginning to take shape with B-24 and B-25 units being transferred into both air forces, along with additional fighter outfits and one Lockheed Lightning photo recon unit each. When the 449th Fighter Squadron arrived in China in the summer of 1943 and the 459th Fighter Squadron in India a few months later, both with P-38s, things really began to look good.

In September 1943, the first Mustangs in the theater – as assortment of P-51As and A-36 Invaders – were attached to the Tenth's 311th Fighter Bomber Group in India. Although an excellent low-level attack aircraft and fighter, the Mustang was not considered an improvement over the P-40 by many pilots. The lightweight P-40N seemed to be the ideal aircraft for the CBI with about the right mix between air-to-air handling and an ability to haul enough bombs and rockets to support the ground troops. The Warhawk was supposed to be outmoded but pilots often found it would take more punishment than the Mustang. Some thought this was due to the lack of a mid-fuselage radiator with the attendant long run of more vulnerable coolant pipes from the engine.

One of the Tenth's most effective units was the 1st Air Commando Group under the joint command of Lt. Cols. Philip G. Cochran and John R. Alison. The Air Commandos entered the theater in February 1944 with twelve B-25Hs, 30 second-hand P-51As, a baker's dozen C-47Bs, another group of C-46s, 100 assorted UC-64, L-1 and L-5 liaison aircraft, 150 Waco CG-4A gliders and four brand-new Sikorsky YR-4 helicopters. The first true composite wing in combat, the Commandos became specialists in unorthodox aerial warfare, using each weapon to its maximum effect, primarily in support of Brig. Orde C. Wingate's Chindits. Specially trained Gurkhas, Burmese and British troops, the Chindits fought a guerrilla war behind enemy lines beginning in February 1943. When the Air Commandos arrived, they were put to work immediately, inserting raiding parties using C-47s with gliders in tow. The fighters and bombers were pinpoint weapons, destroying one fifth of the Japanese air force in Burma within a month, and the liaison aircraft seemed to fly in enemy territory with impunity, picking up and delivering people and communications. Japanese commanders were so harried by Wingate's Chindits and Cochran's Air Commandos, they noted them specifically as major factors in turning the balance of power on the four Burma fronts, thus preventing an invasion of India.

By late 1944, Merlin-powered P-51s, late-model P-47 Thunderbolts and P-61 Black Widows were flying with both air forces. The Fourteenth went on the offensive, attacking Hanoi, Haiphong and even distant Hong Kong. The first B-29 raids were launched from Chengtu in June 1944 but the results were dismal and the aircraft were transferred to the Central Pacific. Regardless of how much effort the CBI air forces expended, the Japanese, with a 1.5-million man army, invaded and took massive amounts of China, often overrunning strong Allied positions, forcing AAF units to abandon their bases, with associated valuable equipment and spares. The CBI was, by all accounts, one of the most difficult in which to fight a war...for both sides.

Air transport operations over the Hump took on gargantuan proportions as the Allied effort increased in intensity. Every organization with a transport aircraft was involved, from combat cargo and troop carrier to the Chinese National Aviation Company and the Royal Air Force, but Air Transport Command (ATC) flew the bulk of the missions. At its peak in 1945, ATC had 725 aircraft and more than 91,000 personnel (including over 5,000 pilots) under its jurisdiction. Although the Japanese sent fighters up to intercept the lumbering, overloaded transports, the real enemy was weather. For the first time in history, aircraft had to fly through severe thunderstorms mixed with heavy icing to make their destinations. Men in combat on the terminus lived and died on the basis of what ATC could get to them, and it cost ATC dearly. More than 1,300 pilots and crew members were lost, along with over 500 transport aircraft. The lessons learned revolutionized the postwar airline industry.

With every Japanese offensive, the two air forces responded with maximum efforts, usually centered around the B-25 units and fighters carrying bombs and rockets. Even the B-24s were called upon to support troops pinned down in tough spots. Japanese shipping was targeted on the Indochina and Chinese coasts from mid 1943 through most of 1944 while enemy-controlled ports were mined, from Haiphong to Formosa. By May 1945, the combined pressure of Allied air power on two fronts, from China and the Pacific, began to squeeze the Japanese out of southern China. The Fourteenth bombed and strafed rail lines, airfields and troop columns all the way into northern China, proving a combined air-ground offensive could win a major campaign. When the war ended, the Japanese still had over 1,000,000 men committed to battle in China.

RIGHT: No matter how difficult the theater of war, nose art appeared on aircraft under even the most trying circumstances. After the 12th Bomb Group was sent from the Mediterranean to the CBI, unit nose artists seemed to step up their efforts. Apparently the farther they were from home, the more determined they became to paint the sides of their Mitchells, like B-25J *Blonde Betty* at Fenny, India. Getting brushes and paint was a major task and the hot sun didn't help either. The metal was often so hot it could not be touched with bare hands. *Hank Redmond*

RIGHT: Bases in the CBI were built by hand, or more accurately, thousands of hands from thousands of local laborers. Here workers, carrying dirt and rubble in baskets on their heads, carve out a strip and revetments at Fenny, India, for the 12th Bomb Group's B-25Hs and Js in March 1944. By April the group was again flying combat, but against a different enemy much harder to find in the thick jungles of Burma, even though front lines were often less than 30 miles away. The Japanese stubbornly held on to vast amounts of territory, forcing Tenth and Fourteenth Air Forces medium bomb groups to cover large areas of trackless green during their missions. Coming back to base was a mixed blessing. Combat flying was dangerous, but it was real flying, while base life in India consisted mainly of living in a tent or "basha" hut. *Hank Redmond*

LEFT: Navigator Hank Redmond (left) sits with a friend in what's left of a 12th Bomb Group B-25 that crashed near the runway at Fenny, India. This poor Mitchell sat for so long in the marshy area it became known as the *Swamp Queen*. Typical of so many World War II types, the Mitchell's rugged construction allowed the crew to get out OK...all the pilots had to do was step out. Due to hard-earned early combat experience, the bombardier and navigator weren't in the nose, which was destroyed, but strapped in behind the pilots with the engineer. The Mitchell's nose gear would collapse under even minor stress (like the failure of the shimmy damper), not to mention hitting holes in a dirt strip. After several personnel, across several different combat theaters, were killed in the nose on landing and take-off, standard operating procedure dictated no one be allowed up there except in flight. *Hank Redmond*

BELOW: The leaders of the 1st Air Commando Group gather in front of bomber section CO R.T. Smith's B-25H *Barbie III*, named for Smith's wife. A former Flying Tiger, Smith stands at the right rear, behind group commander Lt. Col. Philip G. Cochran (right), deputy commander Lt. Col. John R. Alison (middle), Maj. Walter V. Radovich (left) and Maj. Arvid E. Olson (left rear), operations officer and another ex-Flying Tiger. An Ohio State University classmate of cartoonist Milton Caniff, Cochran was made famous as Flip Corkin in Caniff's comic strip *Terry and the Pirates*. Cochran came to the CBI after a tour in P-40s over North Africa, where he shot down three German aircraft. As former 1st Air Commando pilot "Van" Van De Weghe recalled, Cochran "was a pilot's pilot. He would not ask you to fly a mission he wouldn't fly or one he hadn't already flown. He could get his pilots to fly all day, his crew chiefs to work all night and his engineering department to work out details of his fantastic schemes and innovations." *R.T. Smith via Brad Smith*

ABOVE: A 1st Air Commando Group North American P-51A(AC43-6151) Mustang sidles up to the waist window of one of the unit's cannon-armed B-25Hs in 1944. Phil Cochran never met an airplane he didn't think he could use in combat and he thought the Mustangs were more than conventional fighters. He had his engineers bolt cables with heavy steel balls on the end to the wings of these older P-51As, then asked his pilots to rip Japanese telephone wires down with some exceptional low flying. Long before the advent of napalm, drop tanks were filled with used engine oil and fuel, then dropped on enemy ground troops. Following '51s would ignite the mixture with incendiary ammunition. Twenty-inch spikes were attached to the nose fuses of 500-pound bombs and nicknamed "Daisy Cutters" since they blew up above ground, killing and destroying by both shrapnel and concussion. Special bomb racks were fitted to L-5s, not to drop bombs but ammo, food, water and medical supplies to Allied troops in the Burma jungles. The 1st Air Commandos, inspired by their leader, gave birth to a number of techniques and weapons which later became standard. *R.T. Smith via Brad Smith*

OPPOSITE: Fast, maneuverable, with excellent firepower, the Allison-engined Mustang was ideal for the lower altitude combat arena of the CBI, in many ways better suited for the theater than the later Merlin-engined versions. The General Motors Allison V-1710 was less temperamental than its Packard-built Rolls-Royce contemporary. It could run on bad plugs while barely missing a beat, didn't seem to be in great need of tune-ups and could take quite a bit of rough throttle jockeying in combat. The P-51/Allison combination was well liked by pilots and ground crews, something often overshadowed by the Mustang's later Merlin heyday. Former American Volunteer Group ace R.T. Smith stands in front of *Barbie*, his 1st Air Commando Group North American P-51A Mustang. Though Smith was commander of the bomber section and was assigned a B-25H, he was a fighter pilot at heart who talked Phil Cochran into letting him get his share of fighter missions in. *R.T. Smith via Brad Smith*

OPPOSITE: Evaluating the enemy was the job of the Technical Air Intelligence Center (T.A.I.C.) during World War II as it collected enemy equipment from even the most remote areas. This T.A.I.C. Mitsubishi A6M Zero was refurbished, then flown as often as it could be maintained, not only to reveal its engineering but to give American pilots an idea of what they were up against. There was no question the Zero was a superb dogfighter but its light construction, lack of armor plate and no self-sealing fuel tanks made it so vulnerable, only a few well-placed .50-caliber rounds could bring it down. Even so, with an experienced pilot at the controls, the Zero was formidable against more modern types, but that was a rare occurrence. As the war went on, most of the pre-war Japanese pilots were killed or maimed. Replacement pilots had fewer and fewer hours until they were little more than advanced students who knew little about combat tactics. *R.T. Smith via Brad Smith*

LEFT: Navigator/bombardier Capt. Milton W. "Mik" Molakides, with Wabash Cannonball, his 491st Squadron, 341st Bomb Group B-25H Mitchell, takes a break at Yangkai, China in the spring of 1945. One of the first B-25 units in the CBI in early 1943, the 341st immediately encountered the host of problems typical of the theater – bad food, difficult maintenance, heat, malaria, lack of supplies and little mail. But the dreaded monsoon rains took the greatest toll. Torrential sheets of rain, alternating with stifling, penetrating humidity, fostered mold and mildew in barracks bags and foot lockers, spoiled food and ruined cigarettes. Even worse, aircraft, engines and parts rusted and corroded at a great rate. Ground crews soaked engine parts in rust preventative compound and when that ran out, engine oil was used. A monsoon could dump 680 inches of rain in areas of India and Assam in four or five months. In spite of this ongoing nightmare, the 341st and every other Tenth and Fourteenth Air Force unit flew. With the constant harassment of air power, the Japanese were not free to roam across the CBI as they wished, a major reason for eventual Allied victory. *Carroll S. Barnwell*

RIGHT: Bomber pilots dropped under low overcasts, strafed in rainstorms and generally coped with the monsoons while learning the fine points of using the B-25 effectively. After months of hitting rail yards, enemy barracks, ammo dumps, supply depots, airfields and other targets, the 490th Bomb Squadron was directed by its parent Tenth Air Force 341st Bomb Group to make bridges their prime objective. Bridges are very hard to hit, much less destroy, as crews had discovered, but Capt. Robert A. Erdin happened upon something new on January 1, 1944, when going against the Mu River rail bridge. Instead of making a run at an angle, he flew down the rail line at very low level, had to jerk back on the wheel to avoid a tree, and was forced to release his bombs in a slight dive. Instead of bouncing off the bridge, as they usually did, the bombs penetrated the bridge and turned it into a twisted heap. Squadron CO Lt. Col. Robert D MacCarten ordered an immediate training interlude to perfect the technique and, from that point on, the 490th Skull and Wings Squadron became known as the Burma Bridge Busters with one of the highest success rates in the CBI, cutting the enemy drastically short of supplies. This North American B-25G Mitchell of the 490th Bomb Squadron heads across Burma during a mission in 1944. *Edward Branning*

OPPOSITE & ABOVE: After flying ammunition to the surrounded British divisions at Imphal, India, for most of June 1944 to quell the Japanese invasion of India, the 12th Bomb Group went back to bombing. Their efforts were in direct support of Merrill's Marauders (with three battalions and 700 mules), the spearhead of Maj. Gen. "Vinegar Joe" Stilwell's drive to reopen the Burma Road to China and retake the critical airfield at Myitkyina. Indeed, the airfield fell on May 17, 1944, but the Japanese held out in the nearby town until August 5th. For almost the entire month of July, the 12th Bomb Group bombed targets around Myitkyina. On July 23, 1944, these two shots were taken as the group's Mitchells flew their first mission from the newly completed base at Fenny, India, once again hitting Myitkyina. A nine-ship formation, made up of three B-25Js and six B-25Hs, took off at 0915 hours, led by Lt. A.B. Sporer, and though the bombs fell about 750 feet south of the target, Maj. Gen. Davidson at Tenth Air Force HQ sent a message stating "Stilwell delighted on your work today." Lt. R.C. Sauer, flying No.15, had to force land at Imphal when one engine began to run rough. That night, with air and ground crews well settled in at Fenny, a projector was set up in the mess hall and everyone enjoyed watching *Adventures of Tartu*, a real potboiler...but who cared? Hollywood was about as close to home as anyone could get. *Alex Adair*

LEFT: A section of 83rd Squadron, 12th Bomb Group North American B-25J Mitchells heads for targets in Burma, flying out of Fenny, India, in 1944. A few weeks later Lt. Ed Crouch was killed in No.64 when the aircraft was shot down by a Zero making a head-on run through the formation. Japanese pilots, like their German counterparts, learned to avoid most of an American bomber's defensive firepower by making attacks from twelve o'clock. This also had the benefit of targeting the pilots, who had virtually no armor plate forward. To sit in a bomber and watch fighters make head-on attacks, guns winking, took grim, stomach churning courage. The resulting combat fatigue was a genuine malady which affected crews in all theaters, often giving flight surgeons and chaplains more than they were trained for. War in the air was anything but the clean, glamorous, dashing adventure depicted in the comic strips and pulp novels. *Hank Redmond*

BELOW: The Earthquakers, as the 12th Bomb Group had been known since their days in North Africa, were typically called on to perform several different kinds of missions at a moment's notice. After Myitkyina was taken, the group went back to supporting Gen. William J. Slim's British Fourteenth Army, the principal combat force in Southeast Asia. As B-25 pilot Alex Adair recalled, the group began "attacking supply lines, railroad lines and yards, and an occasional river boat, but after a very successful close support mission at a place named Gangau, [Slim] realized how effective we could be on troops and fortifications. We began to get more close support targets. However, because of the distance from our base to the army's targets, we were given a landing field near the recently captured town of Meiktila, Burma, as an advanced base. We could respond in less than an hour to targets given us by the army VCP (Visual Command Post)." This 83rd Squadron, 12th Bomb Group North American B-25J Mitchell taxies to the active runway at Fenny, India, in late 1944. *Hank Redmond*

ABOVE: When the 12th Bomb Group arrived at Meiktila, Burma, the place was in ruins, much from their own bombing. As an 81st Squadron enlisted man wondered, "Perhaps our bombing shouldn't have been so good. Under a well strafed roof, of what was at one time a basha, [we] set up the headquarters of the Operations and Intelligence." Alex Adair recalled, "There were no support facilities near Meiktila, so we sent five combat crews over there to camp out and fly missions with armed and loaded B-25s that were flown over each morning." In spite of the bare facilities, missions from the base were very successful, usually flown between the driving rain storms that fell nearly every day and the constantly blowing wind and sand. This 83rd Squadron North American B-25H-10-NA is being fueled and armed at Fenny, India, prior to a mission in 1944. The 75mm cannon proved quite effective against the non-moving tactical targets found throughout Burma. A pilot and his engineer/loader could carefully plan each squeeze of the trigger. *Hank Redmond*

ABOVE: Without air transport, any effective Allied resistance in the CBI would have been impossible. Not normally assigned the Hump route from India, combat cargo units were responsible for moving men and materiel around inside the theater, keeping the ground and air units viable. Navigating over the forbidding jungle carpet that seemed to stretch to the horizon was a very real hazard, so most theater aircraft were fitted with additional, or new, radio equipment. George "Jake" Saylor looks out the pilot's window of his appropriately named 10th Squadron, 3rd Combat Cargo Group, Douglas C-47 at Kutkai, Burma, near the Chinese border, in 1944. Saylor's Gooney Bird has an additional ADF (automatic direction finder) "football" antenna fairing over the cockpit (there was also one under the nose) as well as a new, state of the art omnirange antenna behind the astrodome. Even fighters had ADF antenna fitted, something rarely, if ever, seen in other combat zones. *George Saylor via Bill Bielauskas*

RIGHT: The runway at Liuchow gets rolled, just like every other field in China, by coolies. Local labor was plentiful and relatively cheap, but it did not come without hazards. Many rural Chinese believed they were hounded by demons, always on their heels, chasing them through life. The massive, powerful aircraft using the airfields seemed ideal for eliminating these pests. On takeoff, pilots would often witness the horrifying sight of one, or more, Chinese dashing in front of their aircraft. Some were hit, most were not. The idea was to sprint across the runway and get on the other side of the aircraft with only a few inches to spare, spelling sure doom for the pursuing demon, which surely would not be able to get out of the way and be hit by this marvelous piece of modern technology. American commanders continually ordered the locals to stop this insane game of chicken, but the practice was never thwarted. It came with having the labor so badly needed to keep airfields operational. *Frederick J. Poats*

BELOW: Though nominally attached to the 23rd Fighter Group, the 118th Tactical Recon Squadron, like so many AAF squadrons, operated independently from several different fields. Originally assigned to the Tenth Air Force flying P-40s from Gushkara, India, in January 1944, the squadron was transferred to China, the Fourteenth Air Force and the 23rd Group the following June. In the process, they converted to the P-51 and its F-6 tac recon, camera-equipped but armed version. Here, 118th Squadron Mustangs at Lao Wan Ping, China, have been readied for a fighter sweep to Hong Kong in June 1945. By this time the 118th often found itself without enough fuel, ammo and spare parts to fly more than a few times a week, sometimes less than that. Keeping the Japanese army in China tied up, rather than defeated, served the same purpose to Allied planners so the war was often quite distant at times. If this fine picture had not been taken more than a half century ago, it might easily be captioned as "Racing P-51s are lined up at Reno for a current event." *Frederick J. Poats*

LEFT: Lt. Fred Poats stands in front of one of the 118th Tactical Recon Squadron North American P-51 Mustangs he flew in combat over China. Though he has a pipe in his mouth, more often than not he had no tobacco for it. With the CBI supply line stretched so thin, such a luxury usually had to come from a friend who would buy a pouch out of theater, then bring it back with him personally. Missions were often a rarity due to lack of fuel so Fred put his time in China to good use by studying local agriculture. The Chinese had been at it far longer than western civilization and Poats found much to consider. After the war he pursued advanced degrees as an agricultural engineer and successfully modeled the Chinese approach for American farmers. It wasn't as much fun as flying P-51s but it certainly yielded an unexpected benefit out of going to war. *Frederick J. Poats*

BELOW: Lao Wan Ping, China, home of the 118th Tactical Recon Squadron and its Mustangs, was not exactly a beehive of activity just before the war ended in 1945. Most of the aircraft on the line here are P-51Ds, as would be expected this late in the war, but many of the Cs were still active since every aircraft in the CBI counted. Newer airframes were supplied all too rarely to consider an older machine substandard. Many experienced pilots who flew the B/C and the D considered the earlier model a better aircraft in many ways – 25 to 50 mph faster in cruise, lighter on the controls, more maneuverable – but the D certainly had far superior visibility, something that would often make the difference in a dogfight. Even so, most of the 118th pilots did not engage in many dogfights since their role was to shoot up ground targets and take pictures of enemy activity. Late in the war there were not that many targets in the CBI. *Frederick J. Poats*

ABOVE: Chinese and American pilots talk over a sortie in front of their Curtiss P-40 Warhawks. Cooperation between the two nations was often strained by the draconian political maneuverings of Chinese leaders, but pilots had to fight a war together, particularly in the Chinese-American Combat Wing (CACW). Initially equipped with P-40s, the wing flew a variety of types, including the P-51, P-47 and B-25, in several different squadrons. Organizationally the CACW was attached to the Chinese Air Force with each aircraft carrying the nationalist blue-and-white sun roundel. The only significant problem faced by the wing's leaders was the assignment of Chinese pilots on the basis of family influence. Some were excellent but others had little or no talent, resulting in some spectacular accidents. By the time the war ended this quandary was sorted out, in large measure, through natural selection and eight of the wing's pilots became aces. *USAF via Stan Piet*

ABOVE: The workhorse of the CBI resupply route over the Hump was the Curtiss Commando, like this C-46A-60-CS. After the Japanese cut off the Burma Road from China to India in early 1942, the only option to keep the Allied war effort in China and Burma going was the genesis of an air transport route from nothing. For the first time in history, pilots had to fly at minimum altitudes of 20,000 feet, in some of the world's worst weather. There was no other choice. As an increasing number of crews were lost and morale went down, Gen. William H. Tunner, who was in charge of the operation, issued an order to force his men to fly: "There will be no weather over the Hump." An average of 700 tons of supplies per month got through, initially under Tenth Air Force command, then the AAF Air Transport Command. A record 71,042 tons was hauled in July 1945 with an average of 650 aircraft crossing the Himalayas each day and over 5,000 pilots on the rosters. By the time it was over, more than 1,300 pilots and crew members were lost and over 500 transports had crashed. *S.I./Groenhoff Collection via Stan Piet*

RIGHT: Ever since its days as the AVG's headquarters, Kunming was the most famous of CBI bases. Not only a center of fighter activity, it was also the terminus of the Hump, so all air activity in the theater revolved around its strategic position. Its fixed facilities were excellent compared to other far-flung bases, complete with revetments, stone barracks and even an officer's club. Even so, nothing, but nothing, could keep the rubble and rocks from being sucked up by spinning propellers and thrown into lowered flaps or air scoops. Anything more than a low-powered taxi setting on the throttle would usually result in some form of damage. Some dings could be ignored as cosmetic, but deep nicks on the prop blades or a gouge in the coolant radiator had to be dealt with immediately. A well-worn 51st Fighter Group North American P-51B Mustang, No.267 of the 26th Squadron, sits in a revetment at Kunming, China, during the summer of 1944. *USAF*

LEFT: Although 12th Bomb Group B-25s at Fenny, India, were ridden hard and put away wet, their nose art was as good as their maintenance. *Oh Dee Whiz!*, one of the group's veteran B-25Js, was always in need of some form of paint touch-up, leading to a patchwork quilt variation of olive drab and neutral gray shading. Olive drab tended to weather ever lighter, particularly in harsh rain and sun climate of the CBI, so when fresh OD was taken out of the can, the resulting mottling effect looked like it was done on purpose. The extra armor plate on the side of the cockpit was effective in combat but a real headache for the maintenance troops. Water, a daily occurrence in India, would run down between the steel plate and the aluminum skin, creating monstrous corrosion. Everything from doped linen to heavy layers of paint was applied all around the plate, but the normal vibration of flight, not to mention the firing of the side pack guns, would break the sealant apart. *Robert E. Wilson via Frederick A. Johnsen*

LEFT: The single Lockheed P-38 Lightning unit in the Fourteenth Air Force (unless one counts the camera-toting 21st Photo Recon Squadron with F-5s), the 449th Fighter Squadron was attached initially to the 23rd Fighter Group in August 1943. Somewhat orphans of the theater, two months later they were transferred to the 51st Fighter Group. Though remaining organizationally attached to this P-40/P-51 outfit, the 449th operated on its own, flying a number of long-range missions from multiple bases. The squadron flew its first missions from Kunming and Lingling, but detachments were quickly sent to Hengyang and Kweilin when commanders found out what the '38 could do. One of the unit's early pilots, Tom Harmon, found out flying fighters was more dangerous than playing football. He went down in the Chinese jungle and walked back to base with the help of locals in several provinces. Before the war ended the 449th flew from another 11 bases, often in detachments which spread the precious Lightnings thin. These 449th Squadron P-38Js rest on the line in January 1945 at Chengkung, where the unit spent most of its time between July 1944 and March 1945. *Frederick J. Poats*

RIGHT: Of this line of 11th Fighter Group, Chinese Air Force, Republic P-47D Thunderbolts at Nanking, most had been transferred from the Fourteenth Air Force's 81st Fighter Group. The American national insignia were quickly painted out by hand and the Nationalist Chinese blue-and-white sun roundels were spray painted on top. There was little time to be elegant with the demands of wartime flying in China. Though the P-47 was not as numerically important in the CBI as the P-40 and the P-51, it was loved by pilots in other theaters of war for the same reasons. Not only could it carry quite a load of firepower, but it was much more rugged than its liquid-cooled brethren. Since the air war in the CBI was, for the most part, a ground attack war, the T-bolt was ideal for the task. *George McKay via Larry Davis*

RIGHT: By the end of the war the Chinese Air Force was well equipped and well trained, with an excellent complement of fighters and bombers serving in several squadrons, including the Chinese-American Combat Wing. There were mixed feelings among all Allied pilots about flying in China since the strategy was to tie up, not specifically to defeat, as much of the Japanese Army as possible. Enemy troops, aircraft and materiel in China could not fight the larger war in the Pacific if they were essentially neutralized. There were long stretches in 1944 and 1945 when Americans and Chinese got very little flying time, much less in combat, because the command structure did not assign any targets. At times this was due to lack of supplies but quite often it was not. Very few combat pilots enjoyed sitting on the ground. Most wanted to get into the fight. This Chinese Air Force North American B-25J Mitchell lifts off at Nanking in 1945. *George McKay via Larry Davis*

LEFT: In August 1945, as the war was coming to an end, the 341st Bomb Group began to convert to Douglas A-26 Invaders at Fenny, India. This 491st Squadron A-26B taxies down, at last, a fairly decent permanent surface which took months of local manual labor to build up. Though the crews loved their new mounts, they never flew them in combat in the CBI. That didn't stop the incredible production pipeline from sending nearly 100 Invaders to the 341st. In October 1945 the group flew these basically brand new aircraft from India to Germany and turned them over to the 344th Bomb Group at Schleissheim near Munich before heading home after a long combat tour. The Invader, certainly one of the more capable wartime aircraft, lasted through two more wars before being retired in late 1969. *Carroll S. Barnwell*

RIGHT: When the war ended, the local inhabitants in all the other theaters of war were left with the task of rebuilding their lives and their nation. The Paris Hotel at Liuchow, China, was nothing but rubble in August 1945, a part of the city targeted by the Fourteenth Air Force on several occasions before the Japanese pulled out. Unlike most other campaigns, the CBI was a constant experience in taking ground, then losing it. Some airfields and towns were lost, then recaptured, then lost again so often, anything of substance was reduced to rubble, then stayed that way. Why rebuild if you're going to have to move out in a month? Tents were pitched amidst the destruction and missions were flown. Since supplies could only dribble in by air, there was no great need for large storage buildings. No question about it, fighting the war in the CBI was very different. *Frederick J. Poats*

OPPOSITE ABOVE: Monya, Burma, was a bustling airfield in 1944 with a strong Royal Air Force contingent of Hurricanes, Spitfires and Mosquitoes. The Spit is a PR.XI, a precious commodity for commanders who needed photo reconnaissance of enemy movements in an almost constant sea of green. Until the arrival of RAF Thunderbolts during 1944, the Hurricane was the RAF's main ground attack fighter in the Far East. During the siege of Imphal, India, in March 1944, six Hurricane squadrons took part in helping the Allies push the Japanese invasion back, doing everything from tactical reconnaissance to killing tanks. The Hurri, in spite of its basic obsolescence, served ably until the end of the war. Ground attack Mosquitoes, operating from bare strips just like the Americans, were fierce weapons with an overpowering forward firing armament of four cannons and four machine guns. *Hank Redmond*

OPPOSITE BOTTOM: The scrap yard at Panagar, India, was quite a depressing sight in late 1945. Though there is a lone B-25 tail section on the right, the rest of the pile is what's left of the 33rd Fighter Group's P-38 Lightnings. Many of these aircraft carried the insignia blue theater bands on their wings and tails. The non-regulation green and gray camouflage on others was clearly applied in country, as was typical of the 459th Fighter Squadron, the other Tenth Air Force Lightning outfit. In the isolated CBI there wasn't much worry about adhering to the letter of the regulations. The idea was to get the job done as quickly as possible. *Frederick J. Poats*

ABOVE: The Whang Po River, winding through Shanghai, China, was quite a crowded place on October 7, 1945, when Americans were trying to make their way home as well as help the Chinese put their country back together. American warships came through regularly, as much for sailors' liberty as for official purposes. In spite of a long, hard war, the city seemed to recover almost overnight. Neon signs went up and commerce, only temporarily underground, came back with a vengeance, driven by 14 years of Japanese intervention and suppression. Sadly, the civil war between the communists and the nationalists would soon draw the war weary Chinese into more fighting and grief. *Maurice J. Eppstein*

ABOVE: While most of the troops had to return home on ships, taking weeks to reach the "good ole USA," some were privileged to come back by air in a day or two on aircraft like this well-kept Douglas C-54G-1-DO Skymaster on the ramp at West Field, Peking. The Air Transport Command had, in the fire of wartime demand, become the most effective logistical air arm in the world. Men who barely knew anything about long-range navigation and cruise control had become masters of reaching even the most remote spots on the globe. This wealth of knowledge gave not only the soon-to-be-born USAF an in-place logistics arm that would fight a new kind of war, but experienced crews gave the airline industry an instant, safe global capability. World War II advanced aviation at least 10 to 15 years up the technological ladder. *David Lucabaugh*

4 FLYING BUCCANEERS

ACROSS THE SOUTHWEST PACIFIC TO THE PHILIPPINES

By mid 1943 the American industrial giant was being turned loose in the Pacific, in spite of the higher priorities of the European theaters. All of the great American wartime fighters and bombers, with the exception of the B-29, and nine new fast aircraft carriers were in combat, manned by well trained crews. Four of the carriers were of the 27,000-ton *Essex* class, capable of carrying over 100 aircraft each.

The AAF's Fifth, Seventh and Thirteenth Air Forces moved up the island chain toward Japan while the Navy's Fifth Fleet assembled its new carriers into task groups. These massive land and sea striking forces required an extensive logistical support chain in the form of an intricate air and sea transport network with mobile supply bases, support facilities, store ships, fuel barges, oil tankers, fixed forward area bases, repair depots and ships, tenders and thousands of men to keep it all moving.

In response to this massive buildup, the Japanese became increasingly more reluctant to send their remaining carriers out and engage the Americans, so they shifted to a strategy relying on land-based aircraft scattered throughout the numerous islands under their control. As their far-flung airfields were reinforced, the number of carrier-based aircraft was reduced to a skeleton complement. This allowed the American carriers to drive hard across the Central Pacific, supported by AAF land-based air, much faster than imagined. The hard-earned lesson of Guadalcanal – gaining and keeping control of the air with a minimum of interservice squabbling – was applied with a vengeance throughout 1943 and well into 1944.

American planners quickly realized they could neutralize, then bypass, certain enemy strongholds. In the summer of 1943 they canceled the invasion of Rabaul, New Britain, then launched a furious series of coordinated Army, Navy and Marine air strikes beginning late in the year to reduce its threat. The two pronged plan was aimed from New Guinea under MacArthur in the Southwest Pacific, with support from the AAF Fifth and Thirteenth Air Forces, and from the Solomons under Halsey in the South Pacific, with support from the Seventh Air Force. The results caused the Japanese to resupply Rabaul with a vengeance, in the process killing off many more of their most experienced pilots and losing thousands of aircraft and ships. Several islands in the Gilberts, including Tarawa, and Bougainville in the Solomons, were invaded in November 1943, then Kwajalein and Eniwetok were taken in the Marshalls.

The Fifth Air Force's Flying Buccaneers flashed across New Guinea, blasting Lae and Finschhafen in September, then dropping

OPPOSITE: When Gen. George C. Kenney's Far East Air Forces moved to the Philippines, the Fifth Air Force's 348th Fighter Group went with it and converted to North American P-51D Mustangs in the process. For most Depression Era kids, flying a '51 was like driving the hot rod they could never afford, or even better yet, an Indy 500 racecar. Of course the Mustang was ideal for rat racing through the clouds and low-level "beat ups" at 300 or 400 mph. Viewed from a B-25 Mitchell, *Betty Lou*, a P-51D belonging to the group's 341st Fighter Squadron, cruises blissfully in heavenly beauty somewhere near its Luzon base in the Philippines, circa 1945. Combat was dangerous, but most pilots couldn't believe the AAF wasn't charging them for the privilege of flying the "wild horses." Like the 58th Fighter Group – flying P-47Ds in the Philippines campaign – 348th Mustangs were decorated with pre-war Air Corps tail stripes, but they were even more striking with vertical fin bands and spinners painted in the squadron color. Since Wilbur Kuhn was there with camera and original Kodachrome, he caught an anomaly on *Betty Lou* which carried 48, a 341st Squadron number, on the fin and yellow 340th Squadron colors. *Wilbur Kuhn via Inez Kuhn*

1,700 paratroopers to capture Nadzab. Kenney's Kids kept pummeling the enemy, bombing and strafing Wakde and Hollandia in March and April 1944 before MacArthur invaded and took the latter stronghold.

Beginning February 17, 1944, Adm. Marc Mitscher's fast carriers hit the major enemy staging base at Truk, in the Caroline Islands, which based over 400 aircraft and served as a major anchorage for the Japanese Combined Fleet. In short order, Navy pilots pummeled Truk to the point it was never again used as a major operating base and the Allies simply bypassed it. The push across the Central Pacific brought the Americans to the Mariana Islands, a very important objective indeed since, from here, the new B-29 could strike Japan itself. The invasion of Saipan on June 15, 1944, was a bloody indication the enemy had no intentions of giving in easily. While Mitscher hit Truk again and other areas in the Marianas, the Seventh Air Force pounded Guam and Saipan. As soon as the Marines took the all-important Aslito Airfield on Saipan, the 318th Fighter Group's P-47Ds were launched from escort carriers, landed, rearmed and began flying combat.

This frontal assault on Saipan finally moved the Japanese to sail from the Philippines with nine carriers to confront their American counterparts, the first time since the Battle of Santa Cruz they were willing to risk their own carriers. When an American submarine spotted the enemy fleet about 900 miles west of Saipan, Adm. Raymond Spruance recalled his carriers from their attack assignments. Concerned the Japanese might divide their forces, as they had in the past, to hit the troops transports and sup-

ply ships involved in the invasion, Spruance ordered Mitscher's carriers to defend Saipan.

Indeed, Adm. Jisaburo Ozawa had divided his force, trying to maximize his 222 fighters and 200 torpedo planes and dive-bombers when facing the 15 American carriers with 500 fighters and over 400 torpedo and dive bombers. Tragically, for Ozawa, most of the men flying his aircraft were barely more than students who had not seen combat, while the Americans were honed to a fine sword's edge. The Battle of the Philippine Sea began on June 19th when Ozawa launched four attack waves. By the time it was over Navy fighter pilots, and anti-aircraft gunners who were now equipped with new proximity fused shells, brought down 373 of 430 attacking Japanese aircraft for the loss of 23 Fifth Fleet aircraft. The engagement was quickly nicknamed "The Great Marianas Turkey Shoot." American subs sank the Shokaku, the fifth of the six Pearl Harbor carriers, and the new 34,000 ton carrier *Taiho*.

The next day, June 20th, Mitscher launched 216 aircraft late in the day against Ozawa's retreating force, sinking the carrier Hiyo and damaging four more. While the Japanese lost 60 aircraft, around 100 American aircraft were lost, most running out of fuel. Fortunately the majority of the crews were rescued. In an unprecedented show of regard for his men, Mitscher risked enemy detection and ordered his carriers' lights turned on after dark to save as many returning crews as possible. Consequently, the Allied invasion forces were free from air attack in taking the gems of the Marianas, Tinian (in late July) and Guam (in early August) which would become major air-

fields for the B-29.

Some of the worst interservice feuding of the war took place over where the Allies would strike next. MacArthur wanted to invade the Philippines while Nimitz was convinced they should be bypassed in favor of taking Formosa, thus cutting the Philippines off from Japan. President Roosevelt himself met with the two commanders at Pearl Harbor in July to settle the issue. After several days of listening to the heated debate, he ordered the invasion of the Philippines.

In June, the Fifth and Thirteenth Air Forces were combined under Kenney into the Far East Air Forces (FEAF), a fitting tribute to one of the Pacific War's most brilliant commanders. In September Allied amphibious forces captured Morotai, a small but strategically important island north of Halmahera between New Guinea and the Philippines, allowing Kenney to strike the East Indies, Borneo with its massive oil refineries at Balikpapan, the Celebes and the Philippines. During the same period, Nimitz was neutralizing the Palau Islands while Halsey's Third Fleet began a series of air strikes against enemy activity in the Philippines in September. When Army and Navy preinvasion air strikes were stepped up in October, the Japanese responded by launching land-based aircraft from Okinawa, Formosa and the Ryukus. Massive air battles were fought for the next ten days but the tables had forever turned as experienced American pilots downed over 500 enemy aircraft, along with a significant amount of shipping. Less than 100 American aircraft were lost.

The Japanese knew they could not afford to lose the Philippines, which protected their southern flanks, thus allowing them to send convoys through the Formosa Channel and the South China Sea without undue Allied harassment. Sending in massive reinforcements, and using Ozawa's carriers as bait, Japanese airmen went after the Allied invasion of Leyte on October 20, 1944, with even more fanaticism. Leyte Gulf became a blood bath, both on the sea and in the air, and the Japanese Combined Fleet was, at last, decimated. Yet, on October 25th, this drove the enemy to launch what Halsey called the most feared weapon of the war, the kamikaze. Twenty-four volunteers from the JNAF's 201st Air Group on Leyte flew their bomb-laden Zeros into escort carriers supporting the invasion, sinking the St.Lo (CVE-63), which took 100 men with her. Two other "jeep" carriers were damaged, this time with help from JAAF pilots who flew alongside their Navy counterparts in the same spirit of suicide for the Emperor.

From the first strips captured on Leyte, AAF fighters and bombers began to hit as many targets as possible, supporting the landings at Ormoc on December 7th and Mindoro on the 15th. By Christmas, Leyte was essentially secured, opening the battle for Luzon with invasions at Lingayen Gulf and south of Manila Bay. American troops were pushing the Japanese out of Manila itself by February. That long-captive city was declared retaken on March 3, 1945. Though the Allies moved on, Gen. Tomoyuki Yamashita refused to give up, fighting with his 65,000 troops in the Luzon hills until the end of the war. The Japanese had intentionally made a wasteland of Manila and many parts of the Philippines, determined to destroy as much of the nation's infrastructure as possible. It would take many years for the Filipinos, with American help, to rebuild their nation.

BELOW: Against a blue sky streaked and spotted with a nice assortment of clouds, a trio of Navy VR-7 Douglas R4D Skytrains out of NAS Jacksonville cruises over serene Florida waters in the spring of 1943 on a mail and supply flight in preparation for combat operations. Douglas cargo/troop carrier/medical airlift aircraft were, with the major support of four-engine, long-range C-54/R5D Skymasters fabricated by the same company, the keys to high-priority delivery of supplies and men. With temporary large-capacity tanks (self-sealing) installed in the cabins, the smaller Skytrains (known by their British name, Dakota, as well) were capable of flying long-range over-water ferry missions. The R4D quickly became indispensable for moving men and materiel across the Pacific. *National Archives*

Often forgotten – or never even understood – was the outstanding part the American airline industry played in every major air freight, troop transport and paratroop operation across all theaters of war. The Curtiss C-46 Commando, like these of the Fifth Troop Carrier Wing being refueled in the Philippines for another mission, stemmed directly from a prewar airline passenger plane, the CW-20T. First flown on March 26, 1940, at St. Louis, Missouri, the prototype was subsequently bought by the Army and designated C-55. As a result of the military expansion program, 46 were ordered for the AAC (Air Corps) in July, but all were to be procured under a C-46A designation – for reasons best known to the procuring agency. Ultimately, and certainly unexpectedly, Curtiss manufactured 3,182 of the impressively large transports – with a wingspan greater than that of a B-17 bomber – in addition to the C-55 prototype. U.S. Marine Corps versions were transferred from AAF stocks at a later date, carrying the designation R5C-1 and being used primarily in connection with the Pacific island-hopping campaign. *Frederick H. Hill*

RIGHT: Thanks to the command intellect and vision of George Kenney, heading the Fifth Air Force, then the Far East Air Forces, and the skills of a great group of highly capable fighter pilots, Lockheed P-38 Lightnings were able to demonstrate their wide repertoire of capabilities in the Pacific War. Twin-engine reliability, heavy firepower (attributable to the foresight of then-lieutenant Ben Kelsey in the mid '30s,) long range and great structural strength in one package proved hard to beat. The unusually large team of mechanics swarming over and under this P-38J or L up on jacks at Lingayen, Luzon, are giving the aircraft a major stage check and refit for its next round of combat missions. *Frederick H. Hill*

LEFT: As the war progressed in favor of the Allied nations, greater numbers of converted bombers were furnished to serve as VIP transports after having reached – for the most part – the status of War Weary. This early North American RB-25D (R for Restricted operation) Mitchell, carrying the incorrect tail number 4129732 instead of the correct 129732, was a prime example of a high-speed executive transport. At Nichols Field near Manila, it featured the early smooth engine cowlings – no short ejector stacks – with a most unusual anti-glare paint treatment and a metalized glass nose. *Bob Kastner*

BELOW: "A picture is worth ten-thousand words," particularly when trying to describe an engine change in the field at Lingayen Airdrome, Luzon, with the gulf just visible beyond the white crystalline sand beach. The PSP (Marston mat) apron is in remarkably good condition, obviously just recently laid down. Engine mechanics uncrate a new Wright R-2600-92 engine, with a normal rating of 1700 horsepower. for this 17th Recon (Bomb) Squadron, Fifth Air Force, B-25J. When compared to some working conditions encountered in virtually every theater of operations just a year or two earlier, this area is neat, clean and well supplied with ground support equipment. *Frederick H. Hill*

ABOVE: Few medium bombers entering combat in World War II, including the vaunted Junkers Ju 88, could boast the firepower of North American's B-25J. Innovative technicians raised the firepower level to new heights never envisioned by the designers or AAF planners and tacticians, and it all initially occurred in the field. In some configurations, as many as fourteen .50-cal. machine guns could be brought to bear on a target during a strafing run. Entire groups were equipped with Mitchells armed to the teeth (figuratively) via retrofit action or as revamped at the factories or at modification centers. At the same time, bomb loads were not seriously curtailed, so mast-level run-in became almost a norm. Routine engine maintenance is being performed on this 17th Recon (Bomb) Squadron B-25J, just about as it would have been in India, Italy or New Guinea. With the waters of Lingayen Gulf rippling in the background, pierced-steel planks, developed for pre-war maneuvers in the rural South and possibly having been fabricated in Henry Kaiser's Fontana (California) steel plant, supported air operations on the sands of Luzon. (First combat use of these Marston mats or PSP was – logically – in the totally contrasting environment of the Aleutian Islands so that fighters and bombers could operate from treacherous tundra.) By V-J Day, PSP was more commonplace in the Pacific Theater of Operations than asphalt or concrete. *Frederick H. Hill*

ABOVE: A line of low-time North American B-25Js assigned to the 38th Bomb Group extends almost to infinity on Luzon in 1945. The hundreds of metal planks comprising a Marston strip appear as a contrasting surrealistic black pathway to the distant mountains. A devastating concentrated weight of bullets from eight, ten, even fourteen .50 caliber guns on some of the Mitchells, often destroyed the superstructure of most any ship up to, and including, light cruisers. Add a couple of well-placed bombs and few of the targets survived. Yellow tiger heads painted on the unglazed noses of 823rd Bomb Squadron B-25s gave enemy crews on deck or on the bridges a preview of the bite they were about to feel. Contrasting soft white clouds against a cool blue sky punctuated by the olive-drab bombers seems unreal – but it was all too real for those exposed to the heavy roar of the .50s and explosions from 500-pound bombs. *Frederick H. Hill*

RIGHT: An assortment of new North American B-25J Mitchells, produced at the Kansas City plant, await assignment and addition of the 17th Recon (Bomb) Squadron's much admired tail markings at Lingayen, Luzon, in the Philippines. At that particular phase of the Pacific warfare scene, eight-gun "solid-nose" B-25s were about the best "attack" category warplanes conceived by AAF/AAC decision makers in a dozen years – despite negativism frequently encountered from the halls of Wright Field. Few understood why Materiel Command/ATSC was reluctant to approve some critical needs, like the emergency procurement and use of Col. Cass Hough's remarkable paper drop tanks in the ETO, then acted like enraptured schoolgirls in the procurement of the Fisher (General Motors) P-75A fighter even as the experimental program revealed terrible design flaws. Fortunately the gun nose Mitchell was born and bred in the Pacific without official oversight. With the weight of ammo slamming into enemy ships, anti-aircraft fire was suppressed, allowing the Mitchells to drop anything from parafrag to armor-piercing bombs with remarkable accuracy. Although the AAF Attack category was becoming a dead issue as the war progressed, the medium bomber in the Pacific became the ultimate attack aircraft. The Douglas A-26 was a bit late in arriving, but its armament arrangements almost immediately mirrored what was already proven by the B-25 in action. *Frederick H. Hill*

LEFT: As defense plant carpool members were prone to say during the war years, "South in the morning, north at night: I wonder where them side roads go?" Well, in the 17th Recon (Bomb) Squadron's Leyte camp, a car would most likely have sunk out of sight in axle-deep, watery side roadways. Fortunately, this four-wheel-drive truck was able to slip-slide its way through the mud of this side road to help get the squadron's job done. Far from the well-paved streets and highways with which they were familiar, whether in the tropics, Italy, Alaska or other remote spots on earth, young Americans and their Allies were faced with unfamiliar trials and tribulations, often maddening, but never impossible. The generation that grew up in the depravations of the Depression had the grit and determination to fight and win a world war. *Frederick H. Hill*

ABOVE: It's almost heresay to refer to this airfield at Eniwetok, Marshall Islands, as a strip. The Engineers had established a basic runway a bit earlier, and it was being used by a Consolidated B-24 to depart on yet another mission in February 1944. Grading equipment was still on the job, widening the original runway by about another 40%, perhaps to permit the multiple/formation takeoffs. What a contrast to "Cactus Strip" on Guadalcanal a couple of millennia earlier...or so it seemed. *National Archives*

ABOVE: *Toddy*, a 531st Bomb Squadron, 380th Bomb Group, Consolidated B-24J-80-CO Liberator, gets a going over in the open at San Jose, Mindoro, in the Philippines, February or March 1945. The 380th was one of Fifth Air Force commander George Kenney's hard working heavy bomb groups which moved up the island chains as the Allies pushed the Japanese back toward the Home Islands. Kenney considered the B-24 an ideal heavy bomber for the long overwater distances of the Southwest Pacific, something he proved in the summer of 1943 when 380th hit the oil refineries at Balikpapan, Borneo, flying 16 hours round trip from Darwin, Australia. The Group became known as The Flying Circus and, in February 1945, each squadron was given a circus symbol to be carried on the upper half of the outboard vertical stabilizers....the 521st carried a seal balancing a bomb on its nose. *Toddy* became the second Lib in the squadron to fly 100 missions, 16 months after it was ferried to Australia in January 1944. On July 5, 1945, after her 111th mission (to Toyahara, Formosa), she was declared "war weary" and pulled off the line. *T.K. Cornwall via Glenn R. Horton, Jr.*

RIGHT: In November 1944, thirty-six of the 21st Fighter Group's twin engine P-38 Lightnings were transferred to the 318th Fighter Group to enhance the Seventh Air Force's long range escort and deep strike capability. The Lighthnings were much loved by the pilots, who flew them in Iwo Jima, Truk and other distant targets until replaced by brand-new P-47Ns. Three former 21st Group P-38L-1-LO Lightnings on the line at Tinian are ready for duty with 318th, normally equipped with Thunderbolts. The 21st never flew their P-38s in anger, using them to fly fighter patrol over the Hawaiian Islands, but did get into the fight in February 1945 with P-51Ds. *Russ Stauffer via Campbell Archives.*

ABOVE: More than a few AAF pilots were thoroughly convinced the Lockheed P-38L-5-LO could take on any contemporary fighter airplane/pilot combination in the world and defeat them. Lightning pilots had the first-ever power-boosted aileron controls applied to a full-production fighter, quick-acting maneuvering flaps, dive flaps and about 1750 available horsepower in each engine for a significant 3400 hp, not to mention an already winning record established by earlier models. Maj. Joseph M. Forster (right) and Capt Lewey J. Noblitt stand next to Forster's late-model 432nd Squadron, 475th Fighter Group L-5, *Florida Cracker*, at Lingayen strip, Luzon in August 1945, just prior to a move to Ie Shima Island. By this time victory over Japan was a fact of life and Forster had nine confirmed victories. Joe had every reason to love the P-38. After getting his fourth victory during the October 14, 1944, mission to Balikpapan, Borneo, a tightly looping Zero shot out his left engine near the target, four hours into the mission. Feathering the prop, Forster flew the 850 miles home to Morotai in 4 hrs, 20 min, which, as far as anyone can figure, was the wartime record for single engine flight in a Lightning. *Joseph M. Forster*

ABOVE: Designed and built as a prototype in a competition for replacement of an obsolete patrol aircraft in the Great Depression years of 1933-1935, the Consolidated XP3Y-1 proved to be an amazing advance in flying boats from the time of its first flight in March 1935. While still located in Buffalo, NY, the company garnered a massive contract for 60 of a slightly revised version redesignated PBY-1 to reflect a new dual function (Patrol-Bomber.) By May 1936, with the company transported to a new factory in San Diego, California, the big flying boat made its initial takeoff from the bay. Ultimately named Catalina and with application – on a grand scale – of the Grumman and Curtiss style retractable landing gear, but with the added feature of a tricycle configuration, the Navy ordered them as PBY-5As. Despite the technicality of having become an amphibious airplane, the PBY was destined to become the most successful flying boat in American history. The USAAF saw a strong need for Catalinas to serve as air-sea rescue aircraft, and ultimately all 230 copies built under license by Canadian Vickers Ltd. as PBV-1As went into the Army as OA-10A-VIs. This one waits on alert in the Philippines with a pair of Lockheed's successful 165-gallon drop tanks, possibly extending the flight duration by 40 percent. A slightly improved model, built by the Naval Aircraft Factory, was designated PBN-1, quietly called Nomads, and most significantly they were pure flying boats. Boeing-built PB2B-2s were nearly identical to the PBNs. *Frederick H. Hill*

133

LEFT: Wonderful Los Angeles county, in 1942, was host to a new shape in the skies on May 26, and co-author Bodie eventually realized he had seen Northrop's XP-61 Black Widow, America's first true night fighter design, on its first flight. Those were exciting days for an 18-year-old transplanted Michigander working on airplanes like the P-70 and C-54 at Douglas Santa Monica. By 1944, Northrop P-61A and P-61B night fighters were deployed to the ETO and POA (in the Far East Air Forces.) A solitary Black Widow taxies on that lengthy Luzon PSP strip populated by B-25Js and Lockheed P-38J and L combat aircraft. Those P-61Bs weighed about 5 tons more than contemporary P-38Ls in service, were about 70 mph slower and took twice as long to reach 20,000 feet. Late series Lightnings could fly 12-14 hour missions, or about equivalent to the Black Widow's ferry range. At the time of Japan's surrender, both types were America's only twin-engine fighters in regular squadron/combat service – P-82s and F7Fs came too late for that duty. All P-61s were night fighters and P-38s were typically day fighters, until two-seat P-38M night fighters were introduced into AAF service near the very end of the war. *Frederick H. Hill*

LEFT: One extremely important military unit operating in the SWPA during the conflict was Technical Air Intelligence Command (T.A.I.C.), primarily involved with retrieval, repair and testing – combined with overall evaluation – of captured enemy aircraft. Performance and construction analysis of these airplanes was of tremendous value in establishing tactical and even logistical countermeasures against enemy operations. This Mitsubishi G4M2a, Navy Type 1 attack bomber (Allied code name Betty), was one of the best bombers operated by either of the Japanese armed services during the war years. Apparently totally overlooked or ignored by pre-December 7th British or American intelligence organizations, early versions were involved in the sinking of the battle wagons HMS *Prince of Wales* and HMS *Repulse*, sailing together from Singapore early in the war without a trace of air cover. The captured Betty, refurbished by dedicated Allied crews to nearly new status at Clark Field, P.I., carries full U.S. Army Air Forces markings, including a set of pre-war tail stripes. *George J. Fleury*

BELOW: Another enemy aircraft left behind at Clark Field, this Kawasaki Ki-45 KAIa Toryu (Dragon Killer, code name Nick) has seen better days, though it's in remarkably good condition. The paint is largely unblemished but all cloth has been stripped from every control surface, most likely the result of American dedication to souvenir hunting. Also, the vertical fin and rudder have been removed from this twin-engine Army Type 2 fighter. Toryu fighters proved to be fairly effective in the defense role against AAF B-24 daylight attacks and, initially, against high-level B-29 daylight raids launched by Twentieth Air Force Bomber Command against the Japanese home islands. Night time low-level raids by the Superfortresses proved to be far more successful for the bombers, far less so for the Nick interceptors. Large numbers of those Kawasaki Ki-45s had been arrayed to defend against the new AAF heavy bombers, but with a top speed directly comparable to that of a Navy Grumman F4F Wildcat and only elementary radar, bomber interdiction was relatively ineffective. *Maurice J. Eppstein*

OPPOSITE: A lineup of several Northrop P-61Bs in the Philippines reveals a mix of Black Widows with and without the dorsal turrets, comparable to those employed on many B-29s in the top, forward position. None of the Black Widows committed to a war zone were equipped with turbo superchargers and were, therefore, medium-altitude fighters. Only a very small number of high-altitude P-61Cs were produced, too late in the war for combat assignments. Probably the great disappointment of the Northrop night fighter program was the extremely long timespan involved in getting the airplane into mass production, then into combat service. When they did get there (mid 1944 in the Seventh Air Force off Saipan), America's first radar-nosed fighter became quite a weapon. Carroll C. Smith, flying with the 418th Night Fighter Squadron, Fifth Air Force, got four of his seven kills during two missions on the same night, December 29/30, 1944, an unequaled feat among night fighter pilots. Three of his kills were scored earler in the P-38, another demonstration of skill considering the Lightnings did not carry radar and were often guided by searchlights, which blinded friend and foe alike. *Frederick H. Hill*

LEFT: Revisionist history can be dangerous. People directly involved in World War II still have a better perspective of events than some who forget who really started the chain of war events. Those who tend to denounce America – frequently from within – for large-scale killing ignore, for example, events in the Philippines in 1941-42 and 1945. More than 40% of Allied prisoners of war captured by the Japanese military forces during the war died in captivity. Only one percent held captive in Germany perished. Fewer than 1/10th of one percent of Japanese combatants (and civilians) captured by the Allies suffered such a fate. That 40% figure does not address a large number of civilians who viewed the war from inside Santo Tomas prison. This is downtown Manila after it was recaptured by American forces. The 1st Cavalry Division, on January 27, 1945, was ordered to drive hard against Manila to rescue internees living in deprivation within Santo Tomas's walls. Landing south of the city, the 11th Airborne Division, operating under good air cover, charged in and rescued 3,400 Americans and others before their captors could put them to death. With more than 15,000 Japanese Marines defending, U.S. forces had to fight a building-to-building onslaught. In the process, much of the city was flattened. *Frederick H. Hill*

TOP RIGHT: A 58th Fighter Group Republic P-47D-23-RA Thunderbolt heads for home with a 75-gallon drop tank still in place after a close support mission to Santiago, North Luzon. No enemy aircraft had been encountered, or the external tank would have been jettisoned. Late wartime markings employed by most Fifth Air Force fighter groups included the wide white-black invasion bands and those wonderful pre-war Air Corps tail stripes. Though the original band markings were supposed to be alternating white and black, to distinguish Allied fighters during the invasion of the Philippines, with natural metal aircraft only two black bands were applied to wings and fuselage...the practice lasted until the end of the war, while the rudder stripes were kept during the occupation of Japan until just before the Korean War. *USAF*

BOTTOM RIGHT: With a cannibalized late model B-24 forming part of the background, a 41st Squadron, 35th Fighter Group North American P-51D on Luzon in 1945 has been deprived of all cowl panels back to the firewall for some fairly serious powerplant and accessory section work. A Beech C-45 Expediter unit hack, displaying pre-war Air Corps tail stripes, is parked next to the "tent city" facilities. The standard "tarmac" or apron for aircraft parking is paved with PSP (pierced steel planks) which served the AAF – in fact, most of the Allied forces – well in even the most remote venues of war. The 35th Fighter Group entered combat with the P-39 and its export version, the P-400, from Port Moresby, New Guinea, in July 1942, then fought its way up New Guinea and several islands to the Philippines, flying P-38s, P-47s and, finally, P-51s. By the time it was over, 35th pilots had downed 397 enemy aircraft. *Frederick H. Hill*

LEFT: Radiating a feeling of "Don't Tread on Me," young, but old beyond his years, Navy Lt.(jg) Joe R. Kristufek was ready to fly and do what came naturally, in a Grumman TBF-1 off the USS *Yorktown* (CV-10), the replacement for the original CV-5, commissioned September 30, 1937. Depression-born CV-5 was lost after the Battle of Midway on June 7, 1942. In those bleak days, pilots like Kristufek were under tremendous pressure to strike, return to the ship, and strike again. And, of course, the Japanese were always trying to send our carriers to the bottom. Unlike the struggling new Vought TBU-1 (later produced in small numbers, with virtually no real success, as the Consolidated TBY-2 Seawolf), the Grumman product was a quick-appearing, substantial winner. Mass produced as the Eastern (General Motors) TBM-3, the Avenger avoided most of the teething problems encountered by so many of its competitors and remained the primary Navy torpedo/attack bomber of the war. *National Archives*

BELOW: A group of bare metal Republic P-47D-23-RA Thunderbolts – and possibly a few -21 or -22 series airplanes mixed in the ranks – are being prepared for allocation to Pacific combat duty. Although factory-new 165-gallon Lockheed-type drop tanks are fitted, the fighters do look a bit shopworn. All have Curtiss Electric propellers installed, but the latest blades had not been supplied. A rather indefinite official caption failed to mention the location, but it could have been Bellows Field, Hawaii, or Clark Field, P.I., both spacious with excellent maintenance facilities at the time. The production record of Republic Aviation compared to the huge Curtiss organization was truly inspiring. Before the war, both Lockheed and Republic were tiny, financially marginal producers held in scorn by the huge kingpin companies. By 1942, the "Lockheed System" of manufacturing was being adopted by the foremost companies, presumably at the "suggestion" of the War Production Board. *USAF*

ABOVE: Hands aboard the USS Missouri (BB-63) had just finished an abandon ship drill in 1944. When the order was sounded throughout the ship, each person had a section of the ship assigned...if even one person was missing, the drill was considered a failure. As the Missouri moved into harm's way, these drills took on increasing importance. That remarkably appealing Vought OS2U-3 Kingfisher was not a very large airplane, but it had to be tough to weather the rigors of catapult takeoffs and landings at sea, exposure to salt spray, and – sometimes – actual combat. Depth charge attacks on submarines were not uncommon. Many downed pilots remembered it for picking them up on the open ocean. The powerplant was the same basic 450-hp engine used in Vultee BT-13/SNV-1 basic trainers. Edo manufactured the floats, but fixed landing gear replaced the sea-going gear for operation from land bases. Production of the Kingfisher ended at Vought-Sikorsky in 1942 following delivery of 1218 versions of the type. The Naval Aircraft Factory delivered 300 copies as OS2N-1s. A somewhat comparable Curtiss observation-scout type, identified as the SO3C-4, was powered by the most unreliable Ranger V-770 inverted air-cooled V-12 engine rated at 450 horsepower. *National Archives*

ABOVE: Curtiss-Wright Corp. and Curtiss Aeroplane & Motor Company, some of the oldest names in world aviation, were hardly luminaries by the end of World War II. While the names of Lockheed, Republic, deHavilland and Avro had grown tremendously in stature, Curtiss had fallen in with Brewster, Miles, Farman Boulton-Paul and Westland....to no happy end. Was that at all attributable to the performance of their line employees? Certainly not. These were the same Americans who worked in war industries over the vast expanse of the continental U.S., largely with sons, daughters and husbands in the service of their country. Management was the culprit - prompted by greed and incompetence at the very least. Curtiss struggled to produce new combat and support aircraft, often like a rudderless ship. Big failures included

the SO3C-4 scout, XF14C fighter, C-76 wooden fall-apart freighter and even their half-hearted attempt to produce Thunderbolt fighters – with minimal success. One other type, their SB2C Helldiver - or more often than not, the "Beast" - finally carried its own weight in the conflict. This wonderful view from "Vulture's Row" of a Helldiver during carrier work-ups in 1943 says a great deal about the rapid growth of carrier aviation, the era of iron men and wooden decks. The prototype XSB2C-1 left the ground for the first time just before Christmas 1940, a month after full production was ordered. It crashed before the holiday and an extensive redesign was ordered. Helldivers were not operational until November 1943, far too long a gestation period.
National Archives

RIGHT: Hardly a recognizable countenance under the best of conditions, the SC-1 Seahawk was the last of a long line of scouts and scout-observation aircraft built by Curtiss. Beginning with the popular SOC-1 Seagull biplane of 1935, all scout/scout-observation types were convertible landplane-seaplane aircraft, capable of being catapulted from battleships and cruisers. Of course they had to be retrievable as well, and that involved being hoisted by crane from the sea off a towed mat to a catapult aboard ship. As it was with the SOC series of naval aircraft, the SC-1 was convertible to fixed (non-retractable) landing gear for operation from airfields. Edo Corporation provided the float gear for all Curtiss SC scouts. Seahawk deliveries began in October 1944, with the first few of 500 operational units being delivered for service aboard the USS *Guam*, the second of three CBs (Large Cruiser class) which were battleship-size cruisers featuring 150,000-hp geared turbines. The sleek CBs were one-third larger than our largest wartime heavy cruisers (CAs). Interestingly, the SC-1 and SC-2 successors were some 40+ mph faster than the single-float Nakajima A6M2-N fighter. That company, already producing Mitsubishi's A6M2 Zero land/carrier fighter, was commissioned to develop a floatplane fighter version of the Zero in 1940. The Navy Type 2 Floatplane Fighter Model 11 made its first flight on the day of our calendar known as December 7, 1941. The code name assigned by the Allies was Rufe. *National Archives*

LEFT: David McCampbell, 1933 graduate of Annapolis, earned his wings at Pensacola in 1938. Hardly a youngster, he got his first kill on June 11, 1944, then shot five aircraft down in a single mission on June 19th during the Marianas Turkey Shoot. As the battles of Leyte Gulf rose to a crescendo, Cdr. McCampbell - flying his F6F Hellcat from the carrier USS *Essex* (CV-9) - led an intercept scramble against a hundred-odd Japanese attackers. He and wingman Lt. Roy Rushing soon "cornered" over 30 of the enemy, who went into a defensive Lufbery circle. As leader of Carrier Air Group 15, McCampbell was going against the rules in this action. In the ensuing fight, he hung up a record score of nine confirmed victories and two probables, setting a standing American record for victories in a single day. Rushing came back with five confirmed. The "game" that day of October 24, 1944 was a fight to the death, with no more than eight F6Fs launched against a mass of incoming attackers. McCampbell was awarded the Medal of Honor for not only his marksmanship, but his leadership, defining the term hero. He ended the war with 34 victories, making him the top Navy ace of all time. *National Archives.*

LEFT: Old timers do need extra care and feeding, and significantly obsolete Douglas SBD-5s most certainly qualified as members of that group. The basic airframe and wing were embodied in a Navy production dive-bomber produced in some quantity as the Northrop BT-1 in the late '30s. Grumman was still delivering their newest F3F-2 and -3 biplane fighters to Navy and Marine squadrons in the spring of 1938 when Northrop began supplying BT-1s to Navy VB-5. In the same time frame, Northrop Aircraft (a Douglas Aircraft subsidiary dating back to 1932) became the Douglas El Segundo Division in 1937, but without the talents of John Northrop who departed to start his own aircraft development company at the end of that year. With further development, the XBT-2 evolved quickly into the SBD-1, all but three or four out of 54 serving with the Marines. It is hard to believe, but as of January 2, 1941, the United States Navy had only 1,913 first-line service aircraft, including those in Reserve Squadrons. El Segundo was still delivering new Dauntlesses in August 1944 as SBD-5s which couldn't exceed 250 mph, even without a war load. In the long run, Douglas produced no fewer than 5,321 of those marvelous "Slow But Deadly" Dauntlesses. *National Archives*

OPPOSITE: In position for a takeoff from the wooden deck of the USS *Yorktown* (CV-10) in 1944, a VT-5 Grumman TBF-1 torpedo-bomber pilot runs up to full power at the direction of the launch officer. Accelerating into the wind, it will pass over the bow and climb out smartly. The Avenger was designed to the general specifications that applied to the old Douglas TBD-1 as a torpedo carrier and sometimes bomber. Most sorties flown by the Grumman-designed Avengers after 1942 were for bombing, sometimes strafing missions. First ordered in 1940, the prototype Grumman XTBF-1 and Vought-Sikorsky XTBU-1 did not appear on the scene until rather late in 1941. The prototype XTBF-1, BuAer number 2539, crashed and burned on October 28, 1941, but the follow-up Avenger (2540) was delivered to the Navy in December as the Pearl Harbor disaster was still rattling our cage. Also braving December temperatures as year end approached, the XTBU-1 Seawolf appeared on the scene in New England on December 20, 1941. Whatever problems overwhelmed the design, many of them had to do with the actual specifications and, unlike its Grumman counterpart, it was much more difficult to produce in quantity. *National Archives*

LEFT: Becoming an ace in wartime was a grim business, no matter what the press releases said. When Lt. (jg) Eugene Ralph Hanks reported to VF-16 and the brand-new USS *Lexington* in January 1943 he had no idea he would become the first Hellcat ace in a day. On November 23, 1943, during a routine combat air patrol over the fleet near Tarawa, Ralph was flying his first mission as a division leader at the head of Red-7 Division, a flight of four F6Fs. Bouncing a formation of over 20 Zeros, the Fighting 16 Hellcats went through and took out several right away. Ralph, in his personal aircraft, No.37, ended up with five of the 17 confirmed victories and one probable during the five-minute fight. Renowned Navy photographer Edward Steichen was aboard ship at the time, so after the five flags were painted on No.37, he snapped this Kodachrome of Ralph in the cockpit. Hanks was actually quite uncomfortable with all the attention, thinking he'd rather be back in Red Bluff, California, showing his prize hogs, which accounts for the grim expression. Ralph got a sixth Zero over Guam on June 19, 1944, during the Marianas Turkey Shoot and after war served two tours with the Blue Angels. *National Archives*

BELOW: Supermarine Spitfire L.F.VIIIs of No. 476 Squadron, Royal Australian Air Force, sit on the line at Morotai, assigned to the South East Asia Command area. Considering the placement of the fighters, there was apparently precious little concern about Japanese strafing/bombing attacks at that stage of the conflict. The L.F.VIII version of the Spit was powered by a 1580-hp Rolls-Royce Merlin 66, giving a maximum speed of 404 mph and a service ceiling of 41,500 feet, right up to and exceeding the standards of the opposition's best. Of course, that altitude performance capability was totally unnecessary in SEAC, but it did provide some nice insurance. The World Absolute Speed Record for aircraft of any type, just a decade earlier, was a shade over 440 mph! The Spit was also the only Allied fighter that could dogfight with the Zero or the Oscar on even terms, quite a valuable capability. *Donald J. Soderlund*

ABOVE: While the United Kingdom appeared to be fighting virtually alone to ward off invasion, surely Col. Carl "Tooey" Spaatz and his aide, Capt. Ben Kelsey, knew the Nazis had an abundance of air transport, and it is unlikely such observations went unreported to Washington. There were very few twin-engine cargo/troop carrier aircraft in American inventory, no four-engine heavy transports and hardly more than a cadre of an air transport system in either the Army or the Navy when the Low Countries were invaded. That in a nation 3,000 miles wide with territories in the far north and well out into the Pacific Ocean. Douglas C-47s were first considered and ordered in 1940. No orders for a four-engine, long-range transport were even in the planning stages until December 8, 1941, if then. Fortunately, Howard Hughes had commissioned Lockheed to build their L-049 Constellation for TWA, forming the cornerstone for the AAF's C-69. Other airlines were the initiators of orders for the production DC-4A, almost immediately after Pearl Harbor to become C-54s. By July 1942, Curtiss – having moved off to at least a start with the C-W Model 20 as the C-55 – was able to start deliveries of C-46s by July 1942. Is it any wonder the Japanese perceived America as being almost totally unprepared for war? Fortunately, by the time this 54th Troop Carrier Wing C-46D was hauling supplies in and out of Lingayen in 1945, the tables had completely turned. *Frederick H. Hill*

ABOVE: When the war ended, the immense American industrial machine and supply pipeline could not be shut off with the wave a bureaucratic hand. All but a few civilian and military organizations were operating at full tilt under the assumption there would be an invasion of Japan, requiring more material than ever, particularly aircraft. With the atomic bombings, things came to a screeching halt, at least in combat. At home, however, the factories were still spewing out metric tons of war making equipment. That's why this Republic P-47N-5-RE Thunderbolt at Clark Field in October 1945 is all dressed with nowhere to go. An auxiliary power unit (APU) stands ready on the left, but there was no war to fight. Pilots did get a few hours a month just to stay current, but the lack of any unit markings makes it obvious the aircraft hadn't even been assigned to a combat outfit. At the time, only the Seventh Air Force was flying N models. Before long this almost-new fighter would be scrapped, a useless weapon of war. *D.Watt via David W. Menard*

ABOVE: By February 1946, Clark Field was a graveyard of combat aircraft, lined up for miles and left rotting in the sun. The P-47Ds were leftovers from the 35th and 348th Fighter Groups which had converted to P-51s before the war was over while the C-46s sat idle with no urgent combat cargo missions awaiting them. British military historian John Keegan has said Americans are unique in the way they go to war. Its as if they are going to work, doing a job they simply want to get over with and go home. They do not want to keep conquered territory or remain the rulers of defeated nations. They want to see the wife and kids, regain the family life they have missed so much and get on with being civilians. Very few wish to be professional soldiers. Keegan said this was the strength of the American ability to avoid military dictatorships. The sad result of this strength is the equipment of war becomes a reminder of combat's horrors so it is quickly scrapped and put out of mind. *Glenn R. Horton, Jr.*

5 PACIFIC SWEEP

Triumph in the Central Pacific, Victory Over Japan

By early 1945 the Japanese empire had been pushed back behind its prewar perimeter with a vengeance burning deep in the soul of the American fighting man. Unfortunately, that vengeance would be matched with a fanatical ferocity which provided every indication the war would be fought to the last man on the home islands themselves. The small islands of Iwo Jima and Okinawa, long Japanese home territory, were the next targets for invasion while the Army Air Forces inflicted flame and fury on Japan itself with Boeing B-29 Superfortress raids.

The United States considered Iwo Jima critical for several reasons. The enemy was using it to launch attacks on the B-29 bases on Guam, Saipan and Tinian, an effort they would surely expand if the island installations were not obliterated. Once captured, it could serve as a P-51 Mustang fighter escort base for B-29s bombing Japan and as an emergency field for battle-crippled Superforts. In November 1944, AAF and USN aircraft and ships began bombing and shelling Iwo. The Seventh Air Force bore the brunt of the effort, launching B-24s and B-25s for 74 consecutive days, the longest pre-invasion bombardment of the war. Among those on Iwo opposing the American aircraft was leading JNAF fighter ace Saburo Sakai, back in combat after losing sight in one eye. His skill at flying the Zero had not diminished but most of his fellow pilots were little more than targets.

On February 19, 1945, the Marines invaded Iwo Jima and some of the bloodiest fighting of the war took place on this five and half by two and half mile spit of volcanic sand. More than 21,000 Japanese soldiers, in 600 pillboxes and gun emplacements, living in a maze of caves, fought virtually to the last man, even beyond March 16th when the island was declared secure. In the predawn darkness of March 26th, the Japanese launched their last Banzai charge, by chance against the newly arrived 21st Fighter Group's collection of tents. Through a chaotic set of circumstances, the defensive positions had been pulled back, leaving the pilots' bivouac unprotected. In short order fighter pilots, mechanics and ground crews were in fierce hand-to-hand combat with a frenzied suicidal enemy. By the time it was over, 15 Americans were dead and 50 more were wounded for nearly three dozen Japanese soldiers killed. Capt. Harry L. Crim, Jr., a 531st Fighter Squadron Mustang pilot to whom this book is dedicated, received the Silver Star for his actions that morning. Undaunted by his introduction to infantry life, he went on to become an ace with six kills and the squadron commander.

The final cost came to 6,821 Americans, moving Nimitz to say that on Iwo Jima "uncommon valor was a common virtue," and 27 Medals of Honor were awarded, more than any single action of the war. Before the fighting was over, a B-29 made the first emergency landing on one of the two airstrips. By the time the war ended, Superforts had pulled off more than 2,400 such landings on Iwo.

Without wasting any time, the Americans headed for Okinawa, only 350 miles from Japan. Both Allied and Japanese strategists con-

A fur' piece from another island – Long Island, New York – a Farmingdale-built Republic P-47N-2-RE lifts its tail for a session of bore-sighting the Browning .50 caliber machine guns. The 19th Squadron, 318th Fighter Group site was about half a world away from the really well-equipped places, so the facilities at this location – Ie Shima Island – were far from lavish, or even hospitable. When the group moved to this small island next to Okinawa in late April 1945 its P-47Ns were committed to escort missions in support of the Boeing B-29 force, but the long-range fighters were soon to take on the mantle of strike-fighters, or probably more appropriately, gunfighters. *James G. Weir*

149

sidered the battle for this central part of the Ryuku Islands the climax of the Central Pacific Campaign since Okinawa would serve as an advanced staging base for the coming invasion of Japan. The enemy was determined to defend it as if it were Nippon itself, but there was disagreement among AAF and USN leaders as to the seriousness of the kamikaze threat from the island. The Navy implored the AAF to concentrate their bomber attacks against the airfields loaded with potential suicide aircraft, but the Army delayed action, a disastrous decision.

The Allied might around Okinawa for the invasion of April 1, 1945, gave some scale to how drastically the two enemies had switched positions. An estimated 100,000 Japanese troops faced around 1,400 Allied ships, 500,000 men and over 1,200 aircraft from all services, including the Royal Navy. As the U.S. Navy had feared, the enemy's great hope was in the dedication and skill of their kamikaze corps, which opened battle immediately by hitting Spruance's Fifth Fleet even before the invasion. On April 6th and 7th the Japanese sent 700 aircraft (half regular dive and torpedo bombers, half kamikazes) against the ships. Not until the grim results were obvious did the AAF send its bombers to hit the Japanese aircraft on the ground.

For the next three months the enemy attack formations ranged from 50 to 300 aircraft at a time, consuming men, machines and ships at an ungodly rate, leading Halsey and Nimitz to consider, at one stage, withdrawing the naval force.

U.S. Navy ships and planes alone claimed 2,336 enemy aircraft destroyed. The ultimate act of suicide came early in the campaign when the Japanese sent the pride of the fleet, their mammoth 69,990-ton-displacement battleship *Yamato*, escorted by nine warships, toward Okinawa with only enough fuel to reach the invasion beaches. Once there, they were to destroy as many American ships as possible before a glorious death. On April 7th, American carriers launched 386 aircraft and quickly sank the force. By the time Okinawa was declared secure on July 2, 1945, more than 107,000 Japanese soldiers and Okinawian civilians had been killed while 31,807 Marines and soldiers were wounded and 7,163 were killed or missing in action. Of 9,731 Navy casualties over 5,000 were killed in action.

Between October 1944 and mid-August 1945, the Japanese launched something like 2,257 kamikaze aircraft against American and British warships. Of these, 1,321 dove toward their targets and 936 turned back. The results were 34 ships sunk (possibly eight of these by conventional attack aircraft) and 368 damaged. The largest vessels lost were three escort carriers, 13 destroyers and one destroyer escort, though several U.S. carriers were knocked out of action, some for the duration of the war. British carriers, fitted with armored decks, fared far better. Of the 6,000 casualties attributed to kamikaze pilots, about half that number were killed. After the war, Chester Nimitz said, "Nothing that happened during the war was a surprise...absolutely nothing except the kamikaze tactics toward the end of the war; we had not visualized these." This was, at last, the final surprise in the American myopic vision of the enemy.

In 1945 the Seventh Air Force joined the Far East Air Forces (which already included its sister arms, the Fifth and Thirteenth Air Forces), creating an even larger AAF aerial armada which began attacking Japan itself from Okinawa and Ie Shima, the small island next to it. Regardless of what they could put in the air for defense, the Japanese had been bled dry of pilots and petroleum. Cdr. Shisei Yasumoto, IJN, one of the defending pilots, recalled, "We could only give new flyers 30 hours of flight instruction because the destruction of the Balikpapan [Borneo] oil complex had drastically cut out training plane fuel allotments. Of 750 training planes, we only had gasoline rations for 180 of them. So by the spring of 1945, we had nothing but raw inexperienced pilots to fight the Americans, and we did not even have many of these. So, defeat became inevitable."

Within the mass of American and British Commonwealth airpower raining destruction on Japan, the B-29 Superfortress was by far the most horrific to the enemy, though it didn't start out that way. After a false start flying from China, the B-29s were moved to the new fields in the Mariana Islands under the command of Brig. Gen. Haywood S. Hansell, Jr., one of the prewar architects of high-altitude strategic bombing war planning. By November 24, 1944, they had made their first raid on Tokyo. The Superfort was plagued with numerous engineering problems, engine fires being one of the most dangerous, but dedicated crews kept it flying. Unfortunately, the aircraft dispatched were not getting enough bombs on target. Since the three billion dollar program, the most expensive of the war, was under the direct control of AAF chief Hap Arnold in Washington, he was motivated by extreme pressure to prove the ultimate bomber was worth the money. In many ways the future of a postwar independent U.S. Air Force hinged on the success of the B-29. Praying for better results, Arnold sent veteran Eighth Air Force leader and original overseas B-29 commander, Maj. Gen. Curtis E. LeMay, to take over XXI Bomber Command in January 1945.

After arriving on Guam, LeMay, in typical fashion, spent six weeks analyzing Superfortress operations, making no changes to Hansell's procedures. The '29 was designed to fly at high altitude, above known (1940) enemy defenses, and destroy targets with far greater efficiency than its unpressurized predecessors. Opposing fighters would be dealt with by remote gun turrets with twelve .50 caliber machine guns. According to the Air Corps Tactical School book, the B-29 should have been murderously efficient. The reality was quite different. The Superfort's service ceiling turned out to be only 31,800 feet while B-17s were good to more than 35,000, and it could carry only 6,000 of its 20,000 pound bomb load on long distance missions. The massive ships were regularly getting less than 5% of their bombs within 1,000 feet of the target, often due to the shifting high winds of the little understood jet stream and cloud cover. Losses were also much higher than predicted.

Going against his experience commanding B-17s in Europe, LeMay departed from the true faith of his bomber colleagues and the Superfort's original design parameters. In early March, he ordered a complete change in tactics to low-level night incendiary bomb attacks from aircraft flying single file and stripped of most of their guns and ammo. A howl went up among his combat crews who were convinced they had been ordered to die in even larger numbers. However, as their ETO colleagues had obeyed such orders before them, they went to Tokyo the night of March 9-10, 1945, displaying as much courage as their commander, who was acutely aware of the risks. A 400-mile-long bomber stream of 334 Superforts at around 5,000 feet dropped 500-pound incendiary clusters every 50 feet. The wood and paper structure-fed fire heated up to 1,800 degrees, lasted four days and burned out 16 square miles of the city, killing 83,793 and injuring another 40,918 while leaving over one million homeless. One-fifth of Tokyo's industrial district was gone, along with two-thirds of its commercial hub, for the loss of 14 aircraft and 42 damaged. No nation could stand such destructive raids for long.

Even more surprising, at least to the crews, were fewer engine fires since there was no long climb to altitude in formation and fuel consumption went down, enabling an even larger bomb load to be carried. Japanese defense forces had far less effective anti-aircraft below 10,000 feet and very few night fighters. Coming back as the sun rose, crews flying crippled bombers could find Iwo Jima more easily, and if they had to ditch, survival and recovery rates went up in daylight. The entire scenario, wholly LeMay's idea and initiated with no approval from Arnold, went against doctrinaire strategic bombing, but he had the courage to discard theory when it didn't work. Those wing and group commanders immediately under him called it suicide, but few people had the intelligence or the tenacity to argue with LeMay.

Of prime importance, however, was LeMay's grasp of Japanese urban organization and construction. These highly populated wooden cities, more densely grouped than those in Europe, would not only burn but they were one massive decentralized production center, where most families built war materiel in their houses. LeMay was well aware he had targeted civilians. As he later said, "I'll tell you what war is about. You've got to kill people, and when you've killed enough they stop fighting.... I suppose if I had lost the war, I would have been tried as a war criminal."

Within ten days, LeMay set the torch to Nagoya, Kobe, Osaka and more of Tokyo. When the campaign went full steam, bombs were used so fast they were unloaded from the dock, driven directly to the line and loaded straight into the bombers. Sortie rates went up until most '29s were flying 120 hours a month, unheard of in the Eighth Air Force in England which, at its peak, was allowing a maximum of 30 hours a month on its B-17s and B-24s. In between the fire raids, LeMay's Superforts still hit industrial targets with high explosive bombs. In a classic strategic blockade, they laid over 12,000 mines in ports, harbors and sea lanes, helping Navy submarines to stop almost all Japanese maritime commerce.

By August 1945, LeMay's men had destroyed 175 square miles of urban Japan in 66 cities, killing over one million and leaving another ten million homeless. Japanese industry vanished. Of the 5,000 B-29 crewmen lost, only around 200 were found alive in Japanese prison camps, a horrendous loss rate when compared with Europe. The overall death rate in Japanese POW camps was 43% versus less than 1% in German camps.

In the midst of this destruction, President Harry S. Truman had to make the decision about using the atomic bomb. The closer the Allies got to Japan, the harder the enemy fought. In spite of the incendiary raids, Japanese civilians chanted the slogan, "a hundred million to die proudly." Fifteen year-old Yukiko Kasai remembered her teacher's instructions: "When the Americans come we must be ready to settle the war by drawing on our Japanese spirit and killing them. Even killing just one American soldier will do." Yukiko was given a carpenter's awl as her weapon. The enemy stockpiling of weapons (over 6,000 aircraft) and men for the forthcoming invasion was a source of great worry to Truman, a former World War I artillery captain who agonized over sending even a single man into battle. The Joint Chiefs' official estimate on possible casualties was around 200,000 while Secretary of War Stimson predicted one million. During the Potsdam conference in July, Truman made his decision, ordering the bomb be dropped no sooner than August 2nd. He later wrote he wanted to "avoid an Okinawa from one end of Japan to another."

On August 6, 1945, 509th Composite Group B-29 *Enola Gay* dropped a single atomic bomb on Hiroshima. Three days later another 509th aircraft, *Bock's Car*, dropped a second atomic bomb, this time on Nagasaki. That afternoon, Japanese Prime Minister Kantaro Suzuki and Emperor Hirohito decided on an immediate peace with the Allies. In his speech of August 15th, Hirohito accepted the unconditional surrender demands without mention-ing them directly, but he did refer to "a most cruel bomb."

Despite an agonizingly slow start after Pearl Harbor, Allied aircraft dropped an amazing tonnage of bombs on targets across the Pacific. The role of Boeing's B-29 can be judged from one significant statistic: from a total wartime weight of 656,400 tons dropped by Allied aircraft, 160,800 tons fell on the home islands. All but 13,800 tons (other AAF aircraft 7,000 and 6,800 by the Navy) of that was carried by B-29s. More than 10,300 Japanese aircraft were destroyed for the loss of 4,530 Allied aircraft. The AAF alone flew 669,235 combat sorties against the Japanese and, at the end of July 1945, had 8,722 combat aircraft – among them over 1,400 Boeings – in Asia and the Pacific.

Had the war not ended in August, the transfer of Eighth Air Force B-17s, B-24s and Royal Air Force Lancasters from Europe, as well as an additional 1,500 B-29s (with 5,000 more on order), would have driven the total Allied heavy bomber force to over 15,000 by the end of 1945. This armada could have dropped as much as 500,000 tons of bombs each month, a fabulous figure considering the monthly average for B-29s from May to August 1945 was just over 34,000 tons.

After the war, Suzuki's predecessor, Fumimaro Konoye, said, "The thing that brought about the determination to make peace was the prolonged bombing by B-29s." Suzuki said almost the same thing. LeMay, firmly in favor of the atomic strikes, agreed with his enemies, later recalling, "The war would have been over in time without dropping the atomic bombs, but every day it went on we were suf-fering casualties, the Japanese were suffering casualties, and the war bill was going up."

The final display of atomic might was a proverbial straw that broke the camel's back. Adm. Asami Nagono, Chief of the Naval General Staff and Supreme Naval Advisor to the Emperor, summed it up...

"If I were to give you one factor as the leading one that led to your victory, I would give you the air force."

OPPOSITE: Dazzling! With her decks loaded with warplanes, the jewels of combat, and wearing a new makeup of dazzle camouflage, the second USS *Hornet* (CV-12) cruises off Okinawa on March 27, 1945, just before the island's invasion. Originally laid down at Newport News Ship Building Co. as USS *Kearsarge* (named after a famous ship of the old Navy) on December 1, 1941, this 27,000-ton *Essex*-class carrier was renamed *Hornet* after the original ship of that name (CV-8) was lost in the Battle of Santa Cruz on October 26, 1942. The earlier 20,000-ton carrier had been a slightly reworked version of the *Yorktown/Enterprise* design ordered in the awful Great Depression year of 1933, but six long years had evaporated before a formal order was actually inked to start work. Fortunately, design activity on those ships initiated in the '30s was a huge improvement over the lightweight USS *Ranger*, a 1929 concept constrained by ludicrous treaty requirements, outgrowths of patriot Woodrow Wilson's ideals and the effects on the world of the War to End All Wars. *National Archives*

OPPOSITE: Close to one year after the debacle at Pearl Harbor, Hawaii, the U.S. Navy was fortunate to have even the one surviving Pacific Fleet carrier USS *Enterprise* (CV-6) in action. It was one of two carriers ordered under the Depression-fostered NRA "Blue Eagle" Act of 1933. Seven CVs (fleet carriers) were on Navy Register on December 7, 1941, but four of them went to the bottom early in combat actions. As the war progressed, no fewer than 17 of the CVs and nine CVLs (Light Carrier Class) reported for duty. Dozens of escort carriers (CVEs) were committed to action, with six of them being lost in battle. This pile of scrap metal is the deck of the USS *Franklin* (CV-13), survivor of a March 19, 1945, attack 50 miles from Honshu, which resulted in two major bomb strikes...the missiles went through her flight deck, loaded with aircraft aft of the bridge, to the hangar deck. The explosions and blast furnace inferno that followed took the lives of 802 men, all in the prime of their lives, and wounded another 265. Incredibly, a month later, on April 28th, the *Franklin* limped back into the Brooklyn Navy Yard near New York City, seen glistening in the background, for major reconstruction. By July 1945, Admiral Halsey's aircrews had bombed the IJN's battle fleets into oblivion. *National Archives*

ABOVE: Good nose art really speaks for itself. Based on cartoonist Milton Caniff's character *Lace*, the reclining lady on this 6th Night Fighter Squadron Northrop P-61B on Isely Field, Saipan, was named *Midnight Belle*. She appears to be at least as large as life and is effectively displayed on the black backdrop. This talented squadron artist, who painted several Widows, was an exceptional copyist, avoiding distortions which often spoiled the work of the original creator. Capt. Mark E. Martin, occupant of that front cockpit from time to time, was quite happy with his red-garbed crew mate. *James G. Weir*

ABOVE: Northrop's Black Widows – at least those sent into operational groups – with their black paint and red AAF tail numbers were certainly something entirely different in American combat aviation. Removal of the top turret with its four heavy-hitting .50 caliber Brownings may have temporarily solved a buffeting problem, but the final P-61As and some 200 of the improved P-61Bs were still plagued with a big penalty. All of that remaining structure, glazing and equipment required to accommodate the turret and gunner added weight and served no real purpose, not to mention the attendant aerodynamic drag. There was very little opportunity to determine if the Lockheed P-38M night fighter would have performed those functions better, but the Lightning was at least 60 mph faster and its service ceiling was more than 11,000 feet higher. These Black Widows, climbing slowly for altitude, represent the final combat version of the AAF's first true purpose-designed night fighter. *USAF via Stan Piet*

OPPOSITE: Late B-series Black Widows like this Philippine-based P-61B-15-NO manufactured in Hawthorne, California, were re-equipped with the 4-gun top turrets after presumably finding a cure for the buffeting problem. Perhaps it would have been possible to produce a lower-drag Widow based on the XP-61D and E versions – which ultimately led to creation of the reconnaissance F-15A – and with even heavier armament to create the epitome of a B-25J Mitchell-like strike aircraft (primarily for the FEAF). Certainly it could have lugged four 2,000-pound bombs on the wing stations for attacking capital warships, or special containers with dozens of parafrag bombs plus up to a dozen zero-length HVARs on other wing stations. The four 20mm cannon in the belly, plus about a half-dozen nose-mounted Brownings, would have been more than deadly. With the Lockheed-type 310-gallon drop tanks at the outboard or inboard wing stations in place of two of the large bombs, range would have been very good, and with all external stores expended, the airplane would have been a reasonably good fighter for self defense. *Frederick H. Hill*

ABOVE: At "zero" feet, a flight of 19th Fighter Squadron Republic P-47D-15-RE and/or -20-RA Thunderbolts head outbound from their 318th Fighter Group base at Isely Field, Saipan. Bearing 75-gallon drop tanks and looking for trouble, these fighters are quite a contrast to the P-47's original design concept as an interceptor and to its high-altitude role in protecting Eighth Air Force bombers from assaults by the *Luftwaffe*. In the Asiatic war, the slugger type was, in essence, flying artillery...even when the long-range P-47N came on the scene. T-bolts, along with their Navy and Marine F4U Corsair counterparts, duked it out "in the weeds" supporting ground troops who kept moving from "one damned island to another," as Pacific AAF vets used to say. *James G. Weir*

ABOVE: The 35th Fighter Group took its Thunderbolts through the long slog up New Guinea, along with the rest of the Fifth Air Force, to Noemfoor, Owi and Morotai, then to the Philippines at the end of 1944. The 41st Fighter Squadron P-47D-28-RA at one of the group's "scenic" bases was flying combat before the strip was finished. With no time for malingering, pilots were no respecters of construction holdups. The old steamroller, so commonplace in the 1930s, quickly gave way to the gasoline- or diesel-engine roller like this one. There is every sign the Allied forces had control of the air, unlike the days at Guadalcanal. Dark tanks – the 165-gallon P-38 type – would possibly have come from Northrop P-61 stocks, but the 58th Fighter Group had embraced their use. The white airfield crushed aggregates were, on the whole, coral which produced an excellent, hard base. On the down side, it was rough on tires, was full of corrosive salt and produced a fine, white dust that got into every-thing, from engines to food. *James W. Althouse, Jr. via James W. Althouse III*

ABOVE: The sun's rays, combined with white coral dust, in the Western Pacific had a Bon Ami scouring powder effect on man and machine. A Douglas C-47/R4D Skytrain/Dakota, carrying unusual red tail numbers, has spent more than its share of time sun bathing at Tinian Island in 1945. The place was enough to give aviation finishes (read that as paint) a bad name. In the face of other pressing needs, fading paint could hardly be fatal. And as far as camouflage effectiveness goes, this Gooney Bird was just trying to emulate chameleons...and rather successfully since markings and paint directives seemed to change constantly and rapidly. If a crew chief left his airplane alone long enough, the current order would change and he'd have enough of an excuse to wait for the next one. *Donald A. Soderlund, Jr.*

OPPOSITE: This 333rd Squadron, 318th Fighter Group, Republic P-47D-22-RE razorback T-bolt, in a revetment on Saipan, was delivered through Bellows Field, Oahu, Hawaii, in May 1944. Many of the Jugs at that staging base were camouflaged, but an almost equal number were in natural dural finish. The black trim on the canopy framework, along with the squadron's distinctive yellow wingtips, tail bands, fuselage band, prop hub and cowling, gave the fighter some character in a very harsh environment. Another quirk was the appearance of Curtiss Electric propellers on so many P-47D-22-REs which were supposed to have been completed with Hamilton-Standard Hydromatic props. Availability in wartime was usually the key to such actions, but nobody ever could say paperwork was 100% accurate. *73rd Bomb Wing Assn. via David W. Menard*

BELOW: Units operating in the Seventh Air Force with Northrop P-61s included the 6th, 548th and the 549th Night Fighter Squadrons, all basically under the control of VII Fighter Command. The 6th Squadron, dating back to the early months of 1917, was armed initially with a mixture of P-70s, P-38s and P-47s, the latter well into 1945. Black Widows in VII FC operated, usually in detachment strength, between Saipan and Hawaii beginning in the first half of 1944. The 548th and 549th Squadrons began as new units equipped with Douglas P-70s in March-April 1944, later enjoying an equipment upgrade to P-61s. *The Spook*, attached to the 548th Squadron, was lost in a night landing accident after clipping a Widow on the flight line. *75th Bomb Wing via Frederick Mollwitz*

ABOVE: Proof that the so-called "Sleeping Giant" of 1941 was wide awake and taking an overdose of NoDoz tablets – the purely American naval seaplane base at Buckner Bay, Okinawa sprang up almost out of whole cloth once the island was taken in 1945. The previous April Fool's Day, the Japanese were firmly ensconced on this small bit of land, ready for one of the fiercest battles of the war. Allied forces – almost entirely American in composition – were on board 1,381 ships of many sizes to participate in landing and supporting 183,000 troops. No fewer than 355 kamikaze pilots attacked during a 36-hour siege that began on April 6, but most were shot out of the skies before they could find their marks. However, so savage was the assault, six Navy ships were sunk and 22 more suffered varying degrees of damage. The battle was over and the island was essentially taken by June 21st, but the toll on both sides was enormous. On the water, extending at least to the horizon, stretch a plethora of ships, and two Martin PBM Mariner flying boats along with a Curtiss SC-1 scout and some carrier aircraft, are resident on the newly created launching ramps. *Robert Kastner*

OPPOSITE: Encountering a Douglas C-54 Skymaster of any model marked with Troop Carrier Command identification stretched along the tubular fuselage was far more uncommon than seeing one with Air Transport Command livery. One TCC Skymaster is being readied for startup at Naha, Okinawa, in the company of several C-46 Commandos cloaked in fading camouflage paint, with an additional C-54 in the background. The long-ranging Skymaster was a real boon to the long logistical chain that stretched across the Pacific. *George McKay via Larry Davis*

RIGHT: Among the most spectacular, innovative, top-quality signboard-sized pieces of nose art in the POA was *American Beauty*, a rendition of Uncle Sam by Cpl. Al Merkling. For some unknown reason, these greatest samples of identity seemed to appear on the co-pilots' sides of bombers as with this 20th Combat Mapping Squadron Consolidated F-7 photo-recon version of the famed B-24. Unfortunately, the F-7 was shot down by Japanese fighters on its twelfth mission. Merkling considered it his masterpiece and the most fun to paint of his creations. *James W. Althouse, Jr. via James W. Althouse III*

ABOVE: The Army Air Forces commandeered the Douglas Santa Monica plant DC-4A production line and the initial 24 United Air Lines and American Airlines airplanes just before co-author Bodie was hired to work on those airplanes...as a trainee...early in 1942. The first three or four DC-4A/C-54 airplanes had been painted and were being finished in preparation for first flights immediately east of the large XB-19 hangar at the time. Test pilot John F. Martin flew the first C-54, AC41-20137, just days after Warren went to work there. The first true military version was the C-54A, manufactured at Santa Monica (Clover Field) and in a new factory located in Chicago, Illinois.

At this point in 1945 seeing a small fleet of Skymasters like these at Hamilton Field, California, getting ready to head across the Pacific, was normal. The C-54G-1-DO nearest the gate lacked any markings relating to the operating command such as ATC or TCC. The G models were the most powerful production versions during the war, employing 1,450-horsepower Pratt & Whitney R-2000-9 engines. A total of 952 Skymasters were rolled out for AAF use, plus another 211 diverted to the USN, designated R5D. *Mark H. Brown/USAFA*

ABOVE: : By 1945 the most numerous of the Grumman-designed Avengers were General Motors Eastern Aircraft Division TBM-3s like these on Okinawa. The airplanes were produced in Trenton, New Jersey, and they were good machines when compared to other naval aircraft produced in the vicinity at Brewster Aeronautical, whose site had to be shut down during America's greatest need. The takeover by the government was caused by the inability of Brewster to produce satisfactory fighting aircraft at any acceptable rate. Grumman, in contrast, built 2,290 Avengers as TBF-1s until early 1944. In the meantime, production was being shifted to Eastern Aircraft which eventually manufactured some 2,882 versions as TBM-1s, then went on to build a very useful 4,664 of the improved TBM-3 model. That plant also manufactured a vast number of Grumman Wildcat fighters as FM-1s and FM-2s, certainly a marvelous cooperative effort in contrast to Brewster's stumbling attempts at producing Vought Corsair fighters under the F3A designation, a situation which finally forced the War Production Board to take action. *Russ Stauffer via Campbell Archives*

OPPOSITE: A gorgeous red-headed woman is a grand sight to behold in any environment, especially at Ie Shima Island in the midst of a war which had all the appearances of rising to a crescendo involving all out invasion of the Japanese home islands. Unfortunately, this redhead was restricted to the cowling of *RED-E RUTH*, Lt. Leon Cox's 19th Fighter Squadron Republic P-47N. The Fighting Gamecocks had a history dating from the days of the 19th Aero Squadron of 1917. The outfit, a part of the 318th Fighter Group, began operating from Ie Shima on April 30, 1945. Cox destroyed three Oscars in quick succession on May 25, 1945. Typical of so many enemy pilots this late in the war, they never tried to maneuver, while some of the Val dive bomber pilots they were escorting made passes at the Thunderbolts, maneuvering violently in spite of carrying bombs. The 19th Squadron P-47s downed the entire flight with very little effort. *James G. Weir*

BELOW: There is plenty of activity on Ie Shima surrounding three up and running 19th Fighter Squadron Republic P-47N fighter-bombers, armed and fueled, ready to taxi. At least one additional T-bolt was moving on the ramp – to the left of the bulldozers – leading from an upper level. All of the 19th's airplanes carried the original fighting cock squadron emblem which had been approved for official use back in April 1928. *James G. Weir*

ABOVE: Late in the war Ie Shima was the center of a great deal of action, particularly for fighters, in the FEAF. The explosion and ensuing conflagration from a 19th Fighter Squadron Thunderbolt, along with another fire in the distance, were hard to ignore, as a 35th Squadron, 8th Fighter Group, Lockheed P-38 hurries down the taxi strip past a Boeing B-17. A very small bit of land only a few miles from Okinawa, Ie Shima seemed to have just about every bit of useable area taken up with aircraft from the Fifth, Seventh and Thirteenth Air Forces, which made up the Far East Air Forces under Lt. Gen. George Kenney. *James G. Weir*

OPPOSITE: Perhaps it was true that gentlemen preferred blondes in numerous haunts, but Capt. John E. Vogt seemed to have a yen for redheads, as his Republic P-47N-2-RE *Drink'n Sister* confirms. Vogt, another member of the 19th Fighter Squadron, became an ace on a single mission, May 28, 1945, when he downed four very passive Zeros over Kyushu, then got one more which had turned to make a pass at the squadron's twelve Thunderbolts. Recurrent, mysterious engine failures were causing far more losses than the enemy, a problem that plagued 318th Group commander Col. Lew Sanders for a long time. Jim Weir, who flew *Weir Wolf* in that outfit, painted most of the squadron's nose art, including Vogt's, then shot several rolls of Kodachrome to record the results. *James G. Weir*

RIGHT: Like a beached beluga whale, this 433rd Troop Carrier Group Curtiss C-46A crashed on landing at Ie Shima in mid 1945. Lights at the end of the newly constructed runway provide a clue to the accident cause. Once into the rough, the outside landing gear – under the load of a sharp turn – collapsed. Fire, a not uncommon factor afflicting Commandos at the time, erupted immediately. Within minutes the C-46 was reduced to a burned-out hulk with flames still licking at the structure (and cargo, perhaps) while shirtless crash crew personnel reconnoiter the hapless wreck. *Jim Gorman*

LEFT: A 34th Squadron, 413th Fighter Group, Republic P-47N ran out of luck at the end of a flight; the trail of oil down the belly shows the pilot had already had a tough time of it – the bent propeller only confirmed the need for an engine change. Fortunately the fire fighters were on the job, hosing down the engine to put out a small fire. An incident like this gave the reflector gunsight an opportunity to do serious damage to an unprepared pilot. That tough Thunderbolt survived to fly another day. *James G. Weir*

OPPOSITE: Lockheed-designed laminar-flow 165-gallon drop tanks were rarely, if ever, utilized on Eighth Air Force P-47s in the ETO, but the Fifth Air Force used them extensively on their P-47Ds as soon as they could obtain stocks. When the N models arrived in the Pacific Ocean Area (which actually ceased to exist as a command in January 1945), those tanks became virtually indispensable for long-range operations. Their value was further enhanced when a full load of napalm and a fuse made the tanks into a widely feared tactical weapon. The 19th Fighter Squadron pilot's choice of a name shows allegiance to a least one USN WAVE when combined with the nose art, painted by squadron pilot Jim Weir, as well as a special vein of patriotism. *James G. Weir*

OPPOSITE: Armed with a pair of 500-pound bombs and four 5-inch HVARs, *Slic Chic*, another Republic P-47N assigned to the 19th Fighter Squadron, is set up for a short-range fighter-bomber ground attack flight. Either the mission didn't require even a 75-gallon drop tank or it hasn't been hung yet. This last version of the Thunderbolt was extremely versatile, able to perform equally well at low altitude helping troops move forward or on very long range bomber escort missions, something that could not be said for the Mustang. When '51 pilots hit the deck to strafe or bomb they knew even a single bullet hole in the cooling system would bring them down in minutes. Pilots who flew the P-47N didn't have the same fear and they found no trouble dealing with enemy aircraft either. Half of the twelve pilots who became aces with the Seventh Air Force belonged to the 318th Fighter Group. *James G. Weir*

BELOW: One of 550 Republic P-47N-5-REs built at Farmingdale, New York, now a part of the 414th Fighter Group, flies close escort for a 6th Bomb Group B-29 over the far reaches of the Western Pacific in 1945. After departing Bluethenthal Field, North Carolina, in June, the Thunderbolts of the 414th settled in at North Field, Iwo Jima, on July 7, 1945. A yellow tail behind a black fuselage band was normally carried by the 413th Squadron's Jugs but a checkerboard cowl ring and side numbers 700 to 749 were assigned to the 437th Squadron. In the thick of combat few ground crews were worried about paint. Originally the 414th, the last P-47 group to enter action, was slated for defensive fighter escort of B-29s attacking Japan, but combat operations only lasted for a month, ending on August 14th. Those missions were limited mainly to strafing and bombing assignments, with the pilots encountering Japanese aircraft only sporadically. By that time, every available Nipponese fighter aircraft was being hoarded to defend against the impending invasion. *John C. Howett*

OPPOSITE: Late war factory-built "solid nose" B-25Js were a real terror to enemy shipping and installations. This particular 823rd Squadron, 38th Bomb Group B-25J-32-NC Mitchell, typical of several aircraft in the group, has but six .50 caliber machine guns in the nose and no fuselage side-mounted package guns. Some pilots preferred to lighten the aircraft up enough to gain some speed and maneuverability while hitting targets at low level. The wing-mounted zero-length rocket launch mounts could be very useful but quite often the unguided rockets gave more drag than lethality. Most 823rd Squadron aircraft were known for having tiger heads painted on their noses. *via Paul Vercammen*

ABOVE: This sad Kawasaki Ki-61-I KAIc Hien, code-named Tony, had suffered several indignities during its short life. These Marines were practicing the age old American art of "chicken plucking" for souvenirs. Before their arrival on the scene at this Okinawa airfield on April 9, 1945, the Japanese Army interceptor had been involved in a crash landing, and that piece of ground support equipment (oil drum) was evidently being used in an attempt to remove the propeller. Like ground crews of all nations, the line mechanics wanted to salvage what they could from the broken hulk but the American invasion of April 1st quickly put an end to things. *National Archives*

LEFT: Hook extended and about to "trap," a square-cut Grumman F6F-5 Hellcat has to take a wave off due to a missed approach or a fouled deck (planes or equipment in the landing area). In the foreground, a pair of dual-mount Bofors 40mm anti-aircraft cannons bristle at the stern of the USS *Randolph.* According to fighter victory historians Barrett Tillman and Frank Olynyk, Grumman Hellcats are credited with destroying 5,221 enemy (less than 100 non-Japanese) aircraft in air-to-air combat, plus an additional 50 or so confirmed destroyed by Royal Navy Hellcats, producing 306 aces. Grumman alone produced 12,275 F6Fs at Bethpage, New York, an astonishing output from one facility. The company developed the new fighter in record time and it turned out to be such a fighting and production success, especially after the company had to empty out Wildcat and Avenger production to General Motors at Trenton, New Jersey, that the Navy considered anything with the name Grumman on it to be gold. *National Archives*

OPPOSITE: There was never any doubt about Republic P-47s being very large and heavy, but F6F Hellcats had a greater wingspan and their gross weights were not drastically less. Both types were pulled along by P&W R-2800 engines, but the AAF jobs had a higher service ceiling (about 6,000 feet higher) with more effective turbosupercharging and larger 4-blade propellers. Conditions in the ETO and MTO demanded maximum possible altitude performance. The Republic P-47M and N were almost exactly 100 mph faster than an F6F-5 at critical altitude, but in the Pacific the Hellcat didn't really need the speed or altitude. These three F6F-5P photo ships attached to VMD-354 were a part of the original detachment that went to Guam in May 1945. The Marine squadron was then based at Peleliu,Ulithi and Okinawa before the war ended. Using armed fighters to carry cameras was an excellent idea since self defense was always a very real worry among reconnaissance pilots. *William M. Derby*

ABOVE: Rapid line maintenance was a constant in all theaters of war. When things went wrong – the nose gear is retracted and there are a few puddles under this 49th Fighter Group P-38L-5 Lightning – American ingenuity effectively compensated for a total absence of ground support, jackstands, or a crane truck. At least two mechanics sit on the horizontal stabilizer, with their backs against the fins, giving the fighter a somewhat aft CG. If the strut, wheel or hydraulics had to be fixed, this was the quickest way. *Lon Hardy*

ABOVE: This brand new North American B-25J Mitchell, sitting in the bright Pacific sun after arrival for combat duty late in the war, will most likely never complete 50 combat missions or get anywhere close to being declared a WW (War Weary). A design initiated in 1939 without a real prototype (a production order for 184 examples was placed in September 1939), the B-25 was a superior aircraft, growing heavier but more potent with age. That initial order was most likely initiated on the basis of FDR's peacetime push for an unprecedented military expansion program. If anybody had any knowledge of his reaction to Army Air Corps/War Department advance planning, it had to include the Army Chief of Staff and top Air Corps chief, Maj. Gen. Henry H. "Hap" Arnold. By 1944-45, the Mitchell was a flying battle cruiser, a medium bomber which far outclassed any Japanese heavy bomber in service. Billy Mitchell surely smiled broadly, wherever he was. *Russ Stauffer via Campbell Archives*

BELOW: There were some good things about an island as airport compared to an aircraft carrier: it didn't roll and pitch during a landing approach or move to a different location during a mission. There were other benefits, but the food would rarely be as good as the food on the large ships. The island of Iwo Jima, with its two airfields, offered fine approaches and safe takeoff zones in the event of engine failure, as well as a critical emergency landing field for B-29s. The engineers and Seabees managed to build first-rate airports in a matter of weeks instead of what would normally take months in a peacetime environment. Parallel runways and close-in facilities promoted multiple operations on round-the-clock schedules when required, which was most of the time. This bit of terra firma may not have rated well as a vacation garden spot in quieter times, but was hard to fault as a base when approaching on a wing and a prayer. *Mark H. Brown/USAFA*

RIGHT: One of the rarest of enemy aircraft, the Nakajima Ki-115 Tsurugi (Sabre) suicide attacker was commissioned as early as January 1945 by the IJAAF for the anticipated defense against invasion of the homeland. It was, in essence, a "tin man." The Tsurugi was adaptable to use a variety of engines with less than 1,300 horsepower, including any new or used engine capable of providing adequate power to fly the aircraft with pilot and explosives. Designed for fabrication by trainable but essentially unskilled laborers, the Tsurugi didn't even have a cockpit enclosure for the pilot. A typical bomb load was 1,764 pounds in this truly "rust bucket" aircraft with no primer paint – left outside for any length of time, the low-grade steel skin would soon be covered with a film of rust. No shock absorbers were provided in the jettisonable landing gear system…really a takeoff system, not intended for a return from its mission. Before World War II, few non-Asiatic people understood the Nipponese predilection for death before dishonor. *George E. Miltz, Jr.*

ABOVE: There seemed to be a hint of Germanic design tastes around the nose, but the amazing functional design advances over the Boeing B-17 and XB-15 bombers of the early '30s, something less than a decade later, were nearly mind boggling. Workable remote gun turrets, where the predecessor B-17s had only two power turrets at the same stage of development, a pressurized cabin and major steps forward with turbo-superchargers on a really fast bomber all contributed to Boeing's advanced B-29 (their Model 345). With the American President solidly behind a program of producing 50,000 warplanes a year and, less publicly, development of an intercontinental Very Heavy Bomber (VHB) program, the Army authorized construction two XB-29 proto-types on August 24, 1940. The fall of France and the Low Countries, then defeat of the British Expeditionary Force on the Continent in June 1941, surely inspired accel-erated development of the new bomber and a backup type – Consolidated's XB-32. The crash of that latter prototype forced the San Diego company to totally redesign the aircraft without retractable remote turrets and a pressure cabin. The Boeing Superfortress effort became the most expensive World War II weapons program at $3 billion. The Manhattan Project came in second at $2 billion. The first XB-29 took off on its maiden flight on September 21, 1942. *Silver Lady* went into combat out of the Marianas with a very long development history behind it. *USAF*

BELOW: Imperial Japanese Army Air Force interception of the Superfortress formations was essentially ineffective, with AAF tactics and the need to rush development of the B-29 being primary causes of higher than anticipated aircraft loss rates and poor bombing results. Ultimately, large numbers of the Superforts were stripped of all but tail turret armament. This permitted an increase in bomb loads which, of course, is the defined reason for the bombing plane to exist. A major switch in bombing tactics was adopted with the transfer of responsibility to a new commander, Maj. Gen. Curtis E. LeMay. High-altitude missions, except for special flight operations, were out and bombing altitudes were brought down to less than 10,000 feet. Night missions displaced daylight bombing while the infrastructure of Japanese manufacturing led to carpet-bombing with incendiary weapons instead of high-explosive bombs. JNAF and JAAF flight personnel were almost totally untrained in night air combat with no realistic night fighter or intercept radar development program. As a result, enemy fighters were quite inefficient at disrupting the bomber formations or crippling the B-29s. *The Strained Crane*, attached to the 501st Bomb Group at North Field, Guam, must have been one of the high-gross weight B-29s, crowding the 140,000-pound level. Night camouflage black paint covers the entire lower portion of the airplane to the centerline of the fuselage. *Mark H. Brown/USAFA*

BELOW: Room with a view extraordinary – the expansive Plexiglas remote turret sighting stations of a B-29, demonstrated by 29th Bomb Group gunner Paul Griber, were excellent at any altitude. As designed, the Superfortress was to utilize Sperry remotely controlled gun turrets, aimed through the use of periscopic sights. At an early stage, the concept called for the same retractable gun turrets as the Consolidated XB-32. The Sperry sighting system with remote turrets worked quite well on the Douglas A-26 at a later date, but the B-29 program could not wait. Therefore, the third XB-29 was tested with the General Electric turret and sighting system where the gunner was located in a sighting station somewhat removed from the low-profile gun turret, making it possible for more than one gunner to have control over a single turret. Each production airplane was G.E.-equipped with four pillbox turrets and a tail turret, normally equipped with two .50 caliber machine guns and a single 20mm cannon. *via Ted Griber*

ABOVE: In the wake of a rainstorm at Naha Field, Okinawa, a disarmed Royal Australian Air Force Consolidated B-24M-10-CO (A72-189) reflects the late day sun's rays. The top turret had been displaced in favor of an additional navigator's astrodome. The first RAAF crews to fly the Lib in late 1943 were attached to the USAAF's 380th Bomb Group in New Guinea. Initially deliveries to Australian squadrons began the next year and by the end of 1945 the B-24 was the mainstay of the nation's heavy bomber force. *David Lucabaugh*

ABOVE: Not to be left out of the military/naval expansion program in 1941, the Naval Aircraft Factory design staff made some improvements on Consolidated's PBY-5 flying boat. This led to a contract award with NAF Philadelphia to build the improved version as PBN-1s, deliveries beginning in February 1943. While that event did not make the newspaper front pages, even more of a non-event was the opening of a new Consolidated factory in New Orleans. In the summer of 1943, the Louisiana factory began to build an amphibious version of the PBN-1, easily identified by a much taller vertical tail, a revised forward gun turret and other improvements, with a new model designation of PBY-6A. This one flew from Okinawa as a photo ship with VMD-354. In addition to 48 of those improved versions being shipped off to the USSR, the Russians ultimately produced an unknown number of the tricycle-gear amphibians, or possibly the PBN flying boat version, in one of their own factories. When production finally came to a halt at Consolidated in April 1945, a dozen years had passed since the Bureau of Aeronautics initial order for the company's P3Y-1, known as the Model 28 in house. In that period, some 2,398 of the Catalinas had been produced by the San Diego-based company. *William M. Derby*

BELOW: USN Martin JM-1 Marauders were normally attached to a utility squadron...as indicated by the "J" prefix in the Navy designation, and the canary-like paint job was a necessity for airplanes then assigned to aerial target-towing duties. The Martin was based in the Pacific to provide ongoing training for Navy and Marine squadrons, as well as anti-aircraft gunners. A few were fitted with cameras for reconnaissance missions, like this JM-1P which was flown by Navy and Marine pilots at Okinawa. These stripped-down bombers were fast...just what the doctor prescribed for target-towing and combat photo recce work. A total of 225 former USAAF AT-23B (B-26C) advanced trainers were transferred to the Navy as JM-1s.
William M. Derby

ABOVE: Camouflage paint on this Curtiss C-46A Commando at Naha, Okinawa, has discolored to a mauve shade, typical of Pacific sun and weather taking their toll on the pigments. Most of the large output of C-46s retained their smoothly faired cockpit windshields, but one XC-46B and seventeen St. Louis-plant C-46Es were built with a new cockpit section having a stepped nose à la Douglas' C-47. One of these C-46Es was tested extensively by the HQ ATC Flight Test Unit – in which co-author Bodie served – at Miami Army Air Field, Florida. After yeoman service in World War II, from the Hump across the Far East, Commandos flew for two years in the Korean "police action" with Combat Cargo Command. But even that was not the final curtain. More served with the 1st Air Commando Group of Tactical Air Command in a counter-insurgency role in Southeast Asia beginning in 1962. *David Lucabaugh*

BELOW: What was a North American P-51D Mustang pilot likely to say upon landing after a lengthy mission to the Japanese mainland and back? This favorite expression, referring to one's aching derrière, is emblazoned on the nose panels of a sleek 21st Fighter Group Merlin-powered fighter. The yellow nose indicates a 72nd Fighter Squadron aircraf. Large wing-mounted drop tanks added approximately 220 gallons of avgas to normal on-board capacity, but proper fuel management was essential in order to maintain a safe CG with that dangerous 85-gallon tank behind the seat. America had been thrown bodily into the war with a most mediocre assortment of combat aircraft, but once the Sleeping Giant was awakened from its dozing pomposity, an avalanche of champion-quality fighters and bombers soon rose to meet the challenge. *Russ Stauffer via Campbell Archives*

OPPOSITE: Although security at Guam, Okinawa and Tinian could not be condemned as slack, the pace of combat and island isolation allowed men to get away with unauthorized use of their cameras. Serious censorship of outgoing packages was, at times, overlooked. Americans treasured their cameras and basic freedoms so they were somewhat adept at completing end runs. The Japanese, before and during the war, enjoyed precious few freedoms for photographic escapades, and German troops had a realistic fear of encountering the Gestapo or diehard SS troopers. As for Kodachrome film, it was rarely available to officials since local processing was near impossible...it had to be sent to Sydney, London or, better yet, Rochester. The new color film in the hands of service personnel with cameras, and a few lucky enough to have exposure meters, was an optimum combination. The war and beautiful sunsets were magnets for these G.I. tourists with their "toy" 35mm cameras, as 29th Bomb Group Superfort crewman Paul Griber discovered at Guam. *via Ted Griber*

RIGHT: Proudly displayed at Ie Shima, the 345th Bombardment Group headquarters sign also carried the emblems of the group's four squadrons, the 498th through 501st Bomb Squadrons. Painted by Sgt. Charles O. Metzel, Group Intelligence, it had been displayed at Clark Field, P.I., before the move to Ie Shima. Group Adjutant Maurey Eppstein points to the blank spot after Ie Shima, wondering where the Air Apaches will go next. Fortunately, the war ended without any other moves. The number of locations was typical of most Pacific War units, which moved constantly as the Japanese were beaten back to the Home Islands. The sign was carefully dismantled, taken home and is still brought to group reunions. *Maurice J. Eppstein*

ABOVE: Certainly one of the most surprising military assets to be seen in the POA during World War II was an example of the 100 Sikorsky R-4B-SI helicopter on Okinawa in 1945. Only a few short years earlier, on September 14, 1939, designer/pilot Igor Sikorsky made a successful first demonstration flight in his VS-300 prototype. It was a success all right, but the Air Corps did not place an order for even one XR-4 experimental example until 1941. Who could assess the possible value of such a machine, particularly on a limited budget? That tube-structure, fabric-covered, 2-seat, dual-control chopper flew for the first time on January 14, 1942. Just a short time later, the XR-4 completed the world's first long-distance cross-country flight while being delivered to Wright Field, Ohio. After small quantities were ordered for service test, the AAF procured a final 100 copies as the R-4B with certain revisions. Other than pilot training and theater evaluation, the lightweight R-4B was not really a fully proven, operational aircraft. On Okinawa it was used for quick parts and personnel runs across the island. *Robert Kastner*

OPPOSITE: Perhaps the Boeing B-29, despite the lean reach of its high-aspect-ratio wing, was function prevailing over form. Yet this single Superfortress lifting off from a crushed aggregate and newly paved runway, against the marvelous cloud backdrop typical of the Pacific, was a beauty to fighting men who knew what it was doing to Japanese war making potential. Whatever imperfections impacted the B-29 airplanes…and there were several…they certainly did better in the advancement scale than any contemporary very heavy bomber under development in Italy, Germany, Japan and even in Great Britain. *USAF*

OPPOSITE: A testimony to her long service, wear and tear had partially eroded the nose art on Boeing B-29-40-BO (AC42-24590) *Celestial Princess*. After 25 missions with the 768th Squadron, 462nd Bomb Group she was declared war weary and sent home in June 1945. Here turrets were removed and she was in need of some serious powerplant systems troubleshooting/repair/engine change as shown by the fully feathered position of the No. 1 Curtiss Electric propeller blades and a work stand already in place. There simply wasn't enough time to solve all the problems on production B-29s. *David Lucabaugh*

BELOW:Red skies at night, sailor's delight. With last light reflecting from its skin, a 315th Bomb Wing Superfortress settles down in the peaceful quiet of the evening on Guam. Either later that night or in the very early morning, it may have roared to life to take on the mantle of a killer – a consummate necessity in the drive to restore world peace. The 315th Wing was assigned oil targets from its first mission, and with the new AN/APQ-7 Eagle bombing radar the results were excellent. *John Worth*

ABOVE: Martin-built Boeing B-29-45-MO *Enola Gay*, named for pilot Col. Paul W. Tibbetts' mother, attached to the 393rd Bombardment Squadron (VH) of the 509th Composite Group, became the most famous Superfortress ever built. The squadron, formed in 1944 with fifteen specially modified bombers intended for missions involving heavy special weapons, moved to Tinian Island, Western Pacific, in 1945. Four B-29s, including the *Enola Gay* loaded with a single 9,700-pound "Little Boy" nuclear device, departed Tinian in the predawn hours of August 6 ,1945 for the first of two atomic bomb raids on Japan's homeland. The massive, unspectacular-looking bomb was dropped at 8:15:17 AM over Hiroshima from 31,060 feet...an altitude absolutely scraping the normal service ceiling of a standard loaded B-29 or B-29A, in spite of two G.E. turbosuperchargers feeding each of the four Wright Duplex Cyclone   R-3350 engines. The equivalent force of 20,000 tons of TNT leveled the heart of the city in an instant. Tibbetts recalled "the whole airplane crackled and crinkled from the blast" while navigator Ted "Dutch" Van Kirk gazed at what looked "like a pot of boiling black oil." *via R. Mann*

OPPOSITE: Perched like a giant bird of prey on its crushed-rock hardstand at Tinian, a 9th Bomb Group B-29 Superfort warms its engines prior to taxiing out for takeoff on yet another mission over Japan. A massive cloud buildup against a cerulean sky makes for a spectacular backdrop to the action just beginning to unfold. The huge production program initiated for delivery of the Very Heavy Bombers (VHB) – as they were officially designated originally – resulted in wartime delivery of more than 2,000 airplanes by August 14, 1945. When the Renton, Washington, production line was closed to B-29 production in May 1946, a total of 3,960 B-29s had been delivered. *Edward C. Vernon*

BELOW: All of the 509th Composite Group's B-29 nose art was extremely well done, including *Bock's Car*, usually assigned to aircraft commander Fred Bock. Flown by Maj. Charles Sweeney with Charles D. Albury as co-pilot and Fred Olivi, Albury's regular copilot, aboard as observer, it headed for Kokura the morning of August 9, 1945. The mission was far more harrowing than intended. Due to a fuel pump failure which trapped 600 gallons of unusable fuel trapped in the tanks, the B-29 was immediately short on range. The weather over Kokura completely obscured the target, forcing the crew to head for the secondary, where they dropped the "Fat Boy" atomic bomb on Nagasaki just after 11:00 AM. Sweeney headed for Okinawa and an emergency landing...as they touched down one engine quit due to fuel starvation. The Emperor's formal surrender came just five days later. The Japanese had their own nuclear development program, which, thankfully, was far from yielding a practical weapon, since they would have used what nuclear devices they had on Allied forces with the same fanatic zeal of the kamikazes. *via R. Mann*

ABOVE: Looking northward from the Asahi Shimbun Building in central Nagoya, the scene is one of appalling devastation as far as the human eye can see. Virtually every gray-cloaked building was not that somber color before the fire-bomb missions called down by Curtis LeMay. The central part of one large red-brick building in the distance is blackened, indicating its usefulness had been obliterated. LeMay believed the fire raids would have ended the war without the atomic bombs, but he was convinced dropping them brought the war to a more speedy conclusion. *Mark H. Brown/ USAFA*

203

BELOW: Tokyo, or Tokio as it was often spelled in those days, looking toward the harbor from the Tokyo Electric Building after the surrender, was little more than a burned out shell. In the distance to the left shipyard cranes are visible but give no clue as to actual conditions at the site; certainly they were not unscathed by the incendiary raids. In the foreground, those vacant ground areas were filled with structures just months earlier. Most masonry buildings standing suffered serious fire damage internally, becoming little more than hulks. During fire storms, the demands for fire-fighting water pressure were overwhelmed, or most fire-fighting equipment was damaged beyond repair. The wind-generating fire storms raged unabated. Over 175 square miles of urban Japan in 66 cities was laid waste, leaving over one million dead and another ten million homeless. *Mark H. Brown/USAFA*

OPPOSITE AND PAGES 206 & 207: A pair of hastily painted white/green cross disarmed Mitsubishi G4M1 Betty bombers flew the official surrender party from Japan to the airfield island of Ie Shima on August 19, 1945. The escort from the Japanese home island had included 49th Fighter Group Lockheed P-38Ls and North American B-25Js from the 345th Bombardment Group. When the Betty "transports" landed and taxied in, thousands of American service personnel lined the runway. Few were at their assigned posts to see this wondrous, almost bewildering, event. At least one escorting aircraft was a Boeing TB-17H Flying Fortress equipped with radar and a rescue lifeboat. When the Japanese emissaries disembarked from their highlighted aircraft, they quickly boarded a Douglas C-54 for the flight to Manila and a meeting with Gen. Douglas MacArthur for surrender terms. *Frederick H. Hill, James W. Althouse, Jr. via James W. Althouse III (2)*

OPPOSITE: Back to the peace the children of Nippon never should have deserted. The beautiful Japanese landscape, dominated by volcanic Fujiyama 12,395 feet above sea level, near Tokyo, was a captivating sight for Allied occupation forces. The conquerors were met with flowers and candy by a people just as determined to obey the Emperor in peace as they were in war. As a result, many Americans formed long-lasting ties with this enemy who had been so brutally savage...the contrast was very difficult for westerners to comprehend. *Mark H. Brown/USAFA*

BELOW: A North American B-25J-27-NC (AC44-30163) with the 498th Squadron, 345th Bomb Group, heads out of Ie Shima Island on August 21, 1945, to escort the Japanese surrender party. The Air Apaches herded the two Mitsubishi G4M1s, painted all white and marked with green crosses, back to Japan. The enemy delegation, led by Lt. Gen. Torashiro Kawabe, had been in the Philippines to work out surrender details. The 49th Fighter Group flew top cover in their P-38 Lightnings. *George J. Fleury*

A sad wasteland of war holds several reasonably undamaged Vought OS2U King-fisher observation-scout seaplanes, obsolete even when flying combat. They were relegated to their last pasture, generally unbent, unholed and only missing a few minor parts. With all major enemies defeated and disarmed, Allied planners knew closed assembly lines could easily be restored to full production in a day or two should the necessity arise (if parts and assemblies had not been destroyed). Command decisions were made to abandon the least needed airplanes where they were, but disabled. The scope of the "quick service" orders were too broad as succeeding generations discovered. A pair of Martin JM-1 Marauders deteriorate in the back-ground, shrugged off and destined to be pots and pans or left where they were. *National Archives*

BELOW: One of three huge Superfortress bases in the Marianas Islands, Guam was the final resting place for many battered Boeing B-29s, along with other aircraft based there. The island was also the headquarters of Maj. Gen. Curtis LeMay's XXI Bomber Command which launched a total of 33,041 bomber sorties from the Marianas and China bases. An astonishing 90% of them originated in the last five months of the war, with a toll of 485 Superforts lost and 2,707 damaged. The bone yard reflects only the worst of those which crashed or returned in damaged condition. The Avenger, almost intact, must have had some serious problems to be tossed into the pit along with several B-24s. *Robert Buchbinder via William A. Rooney*

ABOVE: One of Nakajima's extremely maneuverable Ki 43-II KAI Hayabusa Army fighters was left in reasonably good condition at Kimpo, Korea, after hostilities ended. Evidently the souvenir hunters had managed to loot the luggage compartment door and somebody cut a swatch from the rudder. This type, code named Oscar, was produced in quantity, nearly 6,000 examples having left the production lines. A Nakajima Ki-84 Hayate (code named Frank) rests head-on in the background. In spite of a top speed of less than 400 mph, it was considered a very serious threat against the latest American types. Fortunately for the Allies, most Japanese pilots were so ill trained they became little more than targets for voracious Allied fighter pilots. *Robert Maxwell*

OPPOSITE: Army Air Forces personnel inspecting the Aichi aircraft factory in Nagoya came upon a real surprise, the sleek Aichi M6A1 Seiran (Mountain Haze), an IJN Special Attack Bomber fitted with the company's Atsuta 32 inverted V-12 inline 1,340 horsepower engine. The Allies were totally unaware of this aircraft, which, as a result, was never given a western code name. The Seiran, with complex wing and tail folding, was designed for a single mission, to attack the Panama Canal. Three each were folded and stowed in watertight hangars aboard huge 4,500-ton I-400 or I-401 Class submersible aircraft carriers. Practicing against mock-ups of the Canal's locks and earthen dams, the pilots and sub crews were able, after a long training period, to surface, unfold the aircraft, launch off powerful catapults and submerge in three minutes, totally undetected. After the attack the aircraft were to land next to their mother ships and be recovered. If jumped by enemy fighters, Seiran pilots could jettison the floats, then ditch close enough to be rescued. The floatplanes were not kamikaze aircraft. Allied intelligence was stunned, upon evaluating the plan, to realize the Canal would have been destroyed had the attack taken place. However, due to fear of a possible Allied invasion of the homeland in August 1945, the First Submarine Flotilla was diverted to attack the USN's gigantic anchorage at Ulithi Atoll. While they were at sea Japan surrendered. *Mark H. Brown/USAFA*

BELOW: A miniaturized version of Kingman AAF Base in Arizona, final resting place of many hundreds of surplus warplanes, the Japanese base at Kimpo, Korea, was an aviation photographer's foreign paradise. Two Nakajima-Fokker Super Universal Transports on the left, though built in the '30s and obsolete for combat, served through the war as reliable utility aircraft and crew trainers. Dozens of additional assorted types dot the field, while a lone AAF 160th Liaison Squadron (Commando) Stinson L-5 is parked in the right foreground. Between May 1, 1944 and November 25, 1945, the 160th provided, for the most part, courier service in Korea. With the equipment of a defeated enemy no longer of great interest, no team was authorized to photograph the various aircraft and ground/naval equipment at Kimpo. Had it not been for the amateurs with personal cameras, a famine of historic color pictures would have been global. *Robert Maxwell*

OPPOSITE: A standout attraction on a field of multi-engine aircraft at Atsugi or Irumagawa was this sleek Mitsubishi Ki-46-III two-seat reconnaissance aircraft, Allied code name Dinah, in nearly pristine condition. The most prominent white airplane is a Kawasaki Ki-48-IIa Army Type 99 light bomber, roughly equivalent to a Martin A-30 Baltimore or a Douglas A-20K Havoc. At least two Mitsubishi Ki-21-II heavy bombers (known to the Allies as Sally) with thin coats of white paint and surrender crosses are further down the line. A comparable AAF type in many respects would be the Douglas B-23, never committed to a combat role. One Tachikawa Ki-54c IJAAF light transport and trainer behind the Dinah is more or less comparable to the outstanding Beech C-45/AT-7. Communication with Japanese forces away from Tokyo was so poor the Japanese pleaded with the newly arrived Americans to permit them to use their aircraft for transporting delegations to convince their forces to surrender at isolated outposts. With some trepidation, the conquerors allowed the conquered to fly across Japan, often under heavy American fighter escort, until October 10, 1945, when all Japanese-manned flights were prohibited. In the many hours logged, there were no major incidents. *James W. Althouse, Jr. via James W. Althouse III*

ABOVE: Given the jumbled and battered condition of the airplanes in this bone yard at Ashiya Air Base, Japan, well after the Japanese surrender, even a long-term Lockheed employee from the war years would be hard pressed to recognize the company's P-38s. Their ultimate fate lies in the oxygen and acetylene tanks just visible in the foreground. Bulldozers started with almost-new aircraft, most attached to the 475th and 49th Fighter Groups, and mashed those tough fighters into this wretched mass. It was enough to make a hardened fighter pilot cry. *Harley E. Barnhart*

OPPOSITE: Death Angels with folded wings await their transition into ashes and ingots after yeoman service in the U.S. Navy as great weapons of the Pacific War. Even their identities have been obliterated, with most national insignia painted out. The painters failed to catch the star and bar under the wing of that lonely Douglas SBD-5 Dauntless awaiting its morbid fate after giving all for the home team. Even those Curtiss SB2C "Beasts" would be missed in time, but not by the smelters. Americans as a people go to war as if going to work. They want to get there, do the job, get it over with and go home, leaving the memories behind. These aircraft were only so much junk; consequently any value extracted from them was considered a plus. The average prices, as is, where is, with full fuel tanks, for some of the aircraft on the field...SBD - $1,650; F6F - $3,500; FM-2 - $1,250; J2F - $2,500; PB4Y - $13,750. Veterans had a No.2 priority behind federal agencies and loans were made on aircraft of over 5,000 pounds gross weight...15% down, plus the cost of mortgage insurance, balance payable in 36 equal monthly payments at an annual interest rate of 4% a year on the unpaid balance. For a Corsair at $1,250, that would have amounted to $187.50 down and a little more than $30 a month. Yet, few aircraft were bought at such wonderful terms since not many could afford to feed them. Most disappeared in the smelters. *National Archives*

216

INDEX